Oops! I'm the Paparazzi

a novella

De-ann Black

Toffee Apple Publishing

Published by Toffee Apple Publishing

Oops! I'm the Paparazzi

Large Print Edition

ISBN-13: 978-1-908072-41-2

Toffee Apple Publishing

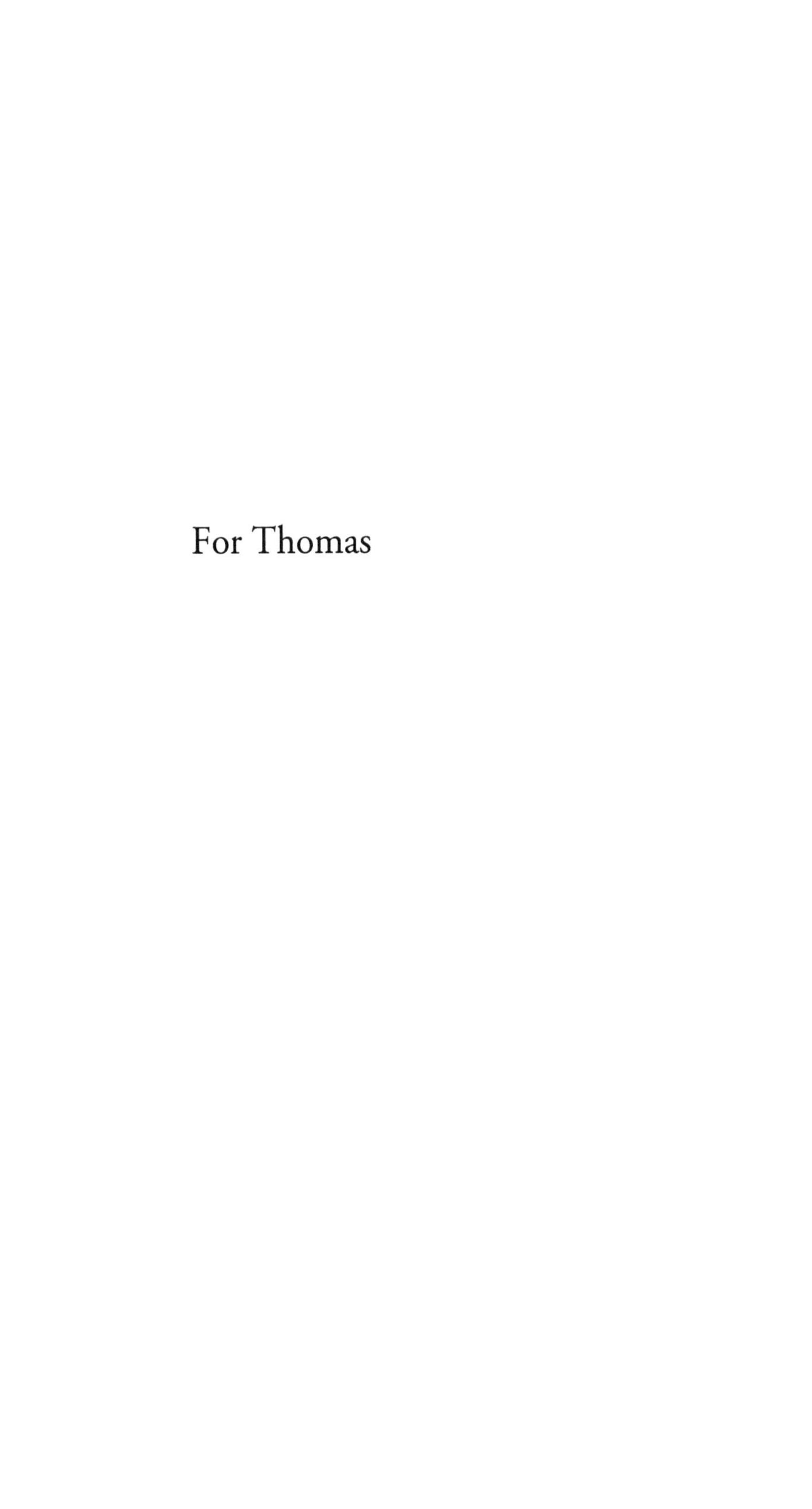

For Thomas

OOPS! I'M THE PAPARAZZI

Contents

Chapter One

One Snowy Night

'I'd rather run off and join the circus than take a cheap handout of money from you!'

These were the last words I'd screamed at Finbar, the so–called love of my life, as he left me completely broke, financially and in every other way. I'd been unceremoniously dumped by my supposed one and only for his one of many.

In hindsight, fate proved to have a sense of humour, because here I was, standing in the centre of bedlam, in the heart of a media circus, otherwise known as a New York newspaper office. One year on, I'd left Dublin city behind and was working in the Big Apple. Though for how much longer I'd actually be employed as a journalist was open to debate.

'Phred! Where the hell is that editorial?'

Ah, the call of the ringmaster. Royce was

the editor who cracked the whip in this particular circus. Then there were the high–wire acts performed by the well seasoned hacks precariously clinging on to their careers by their fingernails. No safety nets in this job.

Over near the window where some real daylight shone in mid–morning were the tenacious sub–editors whose cages you rattled at your peril.

Royce rushed out of his office and charged at me. Although he was from New York, he'd worked for a few years for the press in London, and that's probably where he'd left any shred of finesse. He had a penchant for wearing classic shirts and waistcoats that suited his tall, lean build, and he sometimes wore a burgundy silk backed waistcoat that added to the ringmaster persona. He was also easy on the eye and fairly young in this particular arena. I'm in my late twenties and he's early thirties, but he'd yet to tame the wild streak in me that made me rub his feathers up the wrong way at least once a day. But he liked me. He did. I kept telling myself that.

'Sending it now,' I said and pressed the send button on my computer.

Royce turned and charged back to his office.

Then he popped back out and said to me, 'Is that your hat?'

I paused, jolted into replying, 'Yes.'

He glared at me and shut the door again.

'What's wrong with my woolly hat? It's freezing outside. I paid good money for it in Dublin.'

'It's just *so* not Manhattan,' someone said.

I bit back any remarks and got on with my work. So not Manhattan. Grrr! I knew that my brightly coloured knitted hat with its pom poms and toggles wasn't particularly fashionable, but I was the practical type. It was winter. I was in and out of the newspaper office all day (sometimes all night) chasing one deadline after another. My ears barely had time to defrost in the office before I was sent out again into the frostbitten city. In my world, a woolly hat, scarf, gloves and boots were de rigueur.

Besides, as Finbar had been harsh enough to remind me, no amount of high fashion was going to transform an average little blonde like me into a sex siren. (Bastard). Perhaps that's why I'd been dumped by him and replaced with a string of shiny new models — mainly lithe, long legged brunettes who probably hadn't ever worn a woolly hat. Though I'd dare them to trudge through icy rain and sleet in pursuit of a story. Glamour just didn't come into it.

All was fine for the next twenty minutes — a record in this office. Then Royce emerged from his lair and made a beeline for my desk.

'I need you to do a special job for me. All my paps are down with the lurgy.' (Sickness and diarrhoea to the uninitiated). He handed me an assignment.

I read it quickly. 'You're kidding, right?'

'Nope.'

‘I can’t do this,’ I said.

‘Give me three valid reasons why not.’

‘Well, I haven’t had my conscience removed. I’m a journalist not a photographer, and you’ve given me a complex about my hat.’

Everyone stopped and stared at me.

Royce thrust a camera into my reluctant grasp. ‘There’s the camera, there’s the assignment, and there’s the door.’

It had been snowing all day. Now at almost seven in the evening the urban landscape looked like a winter wonderland. Flakes were still fluttering down from the night sky and everything was glistening in the centre of New York.

All complexes aside, I was glad I’d worn my hat. And my woolly scarf.

When I’d left the office they were running bets on whether I’d get the photograph I’d been sent for. Money was being bet hand over fist. It was the liveliest I’d seen them since yesterday’s deadline. And speaking of money, Royce threw a carrot of enticement into the ring to help ensure I fought like a tiger to bring back the picture they needed. He promised me a percentage of the sale when he syndicated the photograph. I'd love to lie and say I'm not a mercenary when it comes to things like that, but the rent was due on my apartment and cash was tight. Living in New York was an expensive business and most of my wages went on ticking over, making ends meet month to month. Some extra cash would be handy. This was November and winter had already started to bite. I had no one to rely on but myself, so I'd grabbed the carrot along with the camera and headed out into the wintry metropolis.

'Watch your tail,' Royce had said as he closed the door behind me on my way out.

He really had to work on his cheerleading techniques.

I'd been warned that the competition would not be happy if I snatched the winning picture from under their noses, though from the betting odds, I was the rank outsider — a wild card thrown in to take the big boys off guard. Frankly, that was the only hand I'd any chance of winning. Take them off guard, do something totally unexpected, though what that was eluded me as I drove to the scene of the showdown.

My assignment was to glean a candid shot of handsome, rich, sexy, influential, Hollywood star, Bradley Goldsilver, at his latest movie premier. No mean feat. Especially as every other big burly paparazzo with their eye on the money would be vying for the same.

I parked my car near the venue and peered out at the scene.

Crowds were gathered to catch a glimpse of their favourite celebrities outside the premier venue. Film buffs and fans jostled for the best vantage point as near to the red carpet as possible. Awnings kept the snow from falling on the glitterati who posed for the cameras. Television news crews nudged elbows with media hounds armed with flash cameras.

Somewhere in outer space the dazzle from this event was being picked up and analysed by lunar modules.

I took a deep breath, stashed my warm jacket on the back seat of the car, along with my jumper, scarf and gloves. I was wearing skinny grey jeans, a cream thermal vest, black boots, and a determined expression.

I stepped out into the snowy night. The air was freezing.

Numerous paparazzi, many of them large guys carrying step ladders, and some of them already up the step ladders for a better viewpoint, were clicking away furiously. They didn't even notice me. Well, not at first. I had the element of surprise in my favour.

I tightened the loops on my woolly hat, tied them under my chin, and then did something outrageously out of character. Anyone who says a leopard never changes its spots has never worked in the media. Not only did my spots change to stripes, I swear my hat grew devilish little horns.

That photograph was mine . . .

Chapter Two

Pom Poms And The Paparazzi

'Although you could do with some more meat on your bones, you've got a nice little arse and a corking set of boobs on you.' Finbar's rare compliment from the past was the springboard for my plan.

Movie star, Bradley Goldsilver, stood near the entrance to one of the marquees erected outside the main building. They were all done up with fairy lights and posters of Bradley looking mean, moody and sexy in his ripped leather gear. In the posters his blonde hair was precisely ruffled, turquoise blue eyes smouldered, and a faux scar cut across his cheekbone where he'd been injured saving the heroine from the clutches of the bad guys. In real life, Bradley Goldsilver lived up to his name and was a dazzling, 24–carat hottie wearing a white evening jacket that was a perfect match for his diamond–cut smile. A white shirt, white silk tie, and black trousers, completed the ensemble. He was immaculate. Even I swooned a little bit, and he was definitely not my type.

Beside him was his co–star and 'friend' Velvette. The rumour mill hinted of an affair between them, which had been denied by both. Velvette, a sultry vixen, was already married to a Hollywood luminary and any hint of scandal was outrageous. So of course capturing Bradley's hand on her arse was worth a goldmine in headline publicity. But there it was, behind the glitz of the cameras, apparently unseen. Mr movie star's paw had a grip on her peachy posterior. He couldn't resist, and judging by the smile on his sensuous lips, he liked the daring, the chance of being caught, all the while thinking his slight of hand technique was quicker than the eye. And probably it was, especially to the paparazzi guys who were snapping away, unaware of what was going on behind the scenes.

While the paparazzi flashed for all they were worth in one direction, I took a route less obvious, around the side of the marquee, intending to come up from the rear and click the camera into action. There was only one thing standing in the way — about fifty paparazzi whose attention I needed to distract long enough to cut a gap through the middle, take the photograph and then make a run for it back to the car.

I'd planned to take more time, but the opportunity presented itself as I'd stepped out of the car. There was no time to waste. I had to do it now.

And so I did . . .

Rolling up my thermal vest to expose my braless boobs to all and sundry, I ran full pelt in front of the paparazzi. I'd like to think that it was the pertness of my chesticles that made them do a double take and drop their guard long enough for me to snap Bradley and Velvette, but probably my woolly hat had a lot to answer for.

I heard numerous male voices commenting as I ran the gauntlet.

'What the fuck is that chick wearing?'

'What the hell is she doing?'

'Is that a camera she's got?'

'Stop her.'

'Catch her.'

'She's getting away.'

'That's one crazy chick.'

'Sweetest pair of tits I've seen.'

'Did you see her hat?'

'You were looking at her *hat*?'

And I was gone. Hiding in the darkness of the back seat of my car, I wriggled like a contortionist to put my jumper on before scrambling into the front seat and driving back to the newspaper office.

Royce won the bet.

'I knew you'd do it,' he said, and told me to make myself a well deserved hot cup of coffee when I got one for him.

Balancing two coffees and the dregs of a

packet of biscuits, I joined him in his office where I regaled the sequence of events, sans the boob flashing. No one needed to know that.

Royce viewed the photographs on his computer screen while I defrosted, cupping the hot coffee. One of the pictures in particular was bang on the money.

Royce punched the air with his fist. 'Fucking hell, Phred. His hand's so far up her ass he's in danger of losing a cufflink. We'll be printing out hotcakes tomorrow.'

And so that's what happened. The paper hit the streets next morning, the scandal lit the touch paper, sales of the paper soared, and Royce had another assignment for me.

I'd just popped a large chunk of chewy treacle toffee in my mouth when he approached my desk, parking his pert bum on the corner of it.

The first thing he noticed was my hat. I was wearing another hat. Different colours, similar toggles and pom poms.

'You've got another one of those? Do they breed overnight in your wardrobe?'

The homemade chewy toffee slowed down my barbed response.

One of the subs threw a rival paper down on my desk and said to Royce, 'Have you seen this?'

Royce almost choked when he saw what was emblazed across the page — *Woman in woolly hat causes chaos at premier*. A picture of me and my pom poms topped the editorial.

'In my office now!' he roared.

My stomach churned with sheer embarrassment and anger. I hurried after him, and got ready for the slanging match.

He slammed the office door behind me.

'Your tits are headline news! Explain.'

I grabbed the paper and scanned it for any mention of my name. Nothing. 'My face is hidden by the camera. No one will recognise it's me.'

'The hat gives the game away.'

'I wore the hat to keep my hair out the

way of the lens, and to disguise my hair.'

'A large slice of the New York population is now on first name terms with your… pom poms.'

'Yes, but would you have recognised them if I hadn't worn the hat?'

Deep down I was squirming with embarrassment, but I could never show the guys in the office how I felt. I had to brazen it out, pretend it was only a pair of titties. I could freak out later when I got home to my apartment.

One of the reporters popped his head round the door of the office. 'Nice pom poms, Phred, very nice.'

'Out!' Royce shouted at him.

Royce padded up and down his small office like a caged tiger, running his hands through his silky, well cut, brown hair that on occasion I'd had the urge to run my own fingers through. I never did though.

'I can't believe you'd do a thing like that,' he said, sounding exasperated. 'You're always so…so…'

'What? Just say it.'

'Tight ass prudish.'

Well, the home truths were certainly coming out now. So while I was on the ropes I decided to let rip. 'That's rich coming from the man who forced me to cover for the paps. The man who laid bets on me coming back with the photographs, knowing fine that the odds were stacked against me. You could've sent out one of the guys, but oh no, you sent me.'

'I knew you were better than them. You're a better writer too, but I don't know that you're cut out for reporting.'

'What's that supposed to mean?'

'Nothing.' He sank back into his big comfy chair and sighed. 'Sometimes you make me so damn mad I don't know whether to throttle you or kiss you.'

'Don't forget sending me packing back to Dublin. You've used that threat often enough.'

He sighed again. 'I'm all talk, Phred. Don't listen to me. Not that you ever do.'

He pulled the newspaper feature across his desk and studied it calmly. His brow furrowed. And then I thought I saw a glimmer of admiration in his blue eyes.

'Go back to work, Phred. Let things blow over.'

Two dinner invitations, and one to skip dinner entirely and get to the fun part, were on offer when I got back to my desk. I didn't take them up on it, especially as the stinkers had eaten every bit of my treacle toffee.

The day wore on, and the dust seemed to be settling on my pom pom situation when a shit storm reared its ugly head.

'Look who made the early evening news,' one of the reporters said, flicking the sound up on the television in the office. Everyone stopped to watch.

The news team at the movie premier had filmed the whole fiasco. My tits had been blurred so as not to offend teatime viewers. They'd interviewed Bradley Goldsilver.

'It was of course a publicity stunt for the

premier,' he lied, smiling. 'And it worked too. Everyone is talking about what happened. Box office sales will soar.'

'What about you and Velvette?'

'All part of the act. Glad you enjoyed it. Now if you'll excuse me.'

Off he went in a flash of light bulbs.

I could tell from the camber of his shoulders that he was raging mad. I've annoyed enough men in my time to know that stance. Thankfully, our paths were never likely to cross again.

I was eating an iced doughnut and drinking tea in my car outside the newspaper building (away from the constant ribbing in the office) when someone knocked on the window. It was one of the subs.

'Bradley Goldsilver is hunting you down.'

'What?'

'There's money being offered to any of the paparazzi who know your name and address.'

'None of the paparazzi know me.'

His expression darkened. 'Someone in the paper has ratted you out. Wasn't me. Big bucks were paid for the information. Better it was one of us rather than someone else, huh?'

'Isn't that just heart–warming.'

'Sorry, Phred.'

I drove home. The snow was getting heavier. By the time I arrived outside my apartment, the cars in the street were covered in it. I stepped out, feeling my boots crunch into the drifts. I was so busy trying to collect my bag and laptop, I barely noticed the man standing nearby.

'I'd like to talk to you, Phred,' he called out.

I turned around at the sound of the voice and there was Bradley Goldsilver standing in the street beneath a lamp post. Even out of situ this man still found a spotlight to shine on him, deliberate or not.

His cashmere coat was pale cream, the collar turned up against the cold, and flakes of snow fell like icy stardust on his blonde hair.

‘Can we talk inside?’ he said.

‘Inside my apartment?’

He nodded. ‘Or we can drive to my house,’ he said, glancing at his silver limousine that was bigger than my kitchen.

Neither of us was fudging the issue. We both knew what I’d done. Maybe not all the details but the basics were pretty clear. I’d caught him red handed. He’d wriggled off the hook and Velvette’s honour was safe. No real harm had been done. The press and the premier had both benefited from the publicity.

‘I don’t usually fete the paparazzi,’ he said.

‘I’m not really the paparazzi.’

‘No? You work for the press. You’re a newspaper journalist. You go to movie premiers and take photographs with press cameras, and the pictures are published in the media. Sounds like the paparazzi to me.’

I wasn’t going to argue, especially as I’d agreed to another two assignments for tonight from Royce.

'Can we go inside before we freeze to death?' he said.

I fished out my door key from my bag and hoped the apartment didn't throw further shame on my character. Thankfully it looked clean and tidy although perhaps a bit sparse of luxuries.

Seeing Bradley step into my lounge was a strange experience. Frankly, I've never been one to be starstruck, but there was something about this beautiful, immaculate man that made me look in wonder at him standing there. But I think I hid my reaction. I did. I'm sure I did.

'You live here?' It wasn't so much a question for me, rather a sounding board for himself that someone actually lived in such a small, bleak environment.

'For the moment. Nothing's permanent.'

'Why not?'

'Because I'm from Dublin, and I'm trying to see how things work out for me in New York. Whether I'll be turfed back to where I came from, or move on and better myself.'

'And how would you better yourself? By becoming an editor?'

'No, I'd like to be a writer.'

'Not a newspaper journalist then?'

'Not forever, no.'

'What sort of writer? A novelist? Playwright?'

'Scriptwriter.'

He viewed me sceptically. 'Are you any good?'

'Maybe.'

He nodded.

'My plan is to keep making movies,' he said.

'Like the ones you make just now?'

'Yes, why? Is there something in their success that you find distasteful?'

'No, I just think you're selling yourself short. But what do I know about acting?'

'You think I'm a bad actor?'

'Not at all. That's the problem. I think

you're wasted on the movies you make.'

'You'd have me make other types of movies?'

'Yes.'

'What sort?'

'A romantic comedy perhaps or a classic spy thriller. Something different from your usual special effects sci–fi films.'

'Hmm,' was all he said.

'You wanted to talk to me?' I said, breaking the awkward moment.

'Yes. I wanted to ask you if there are any other photographs of me that I should be wary of being published in the press?'

'Not from me.'

He nodded, seeming to take me at my word.

He looked around. 'It's freezing in here.'

'I only put the heating on when I'm home, and I've been out all day.'

He glanced at me as if this troubled him.

'I assume you have family back home in Dublin.'

'No. There's no one but me.'

He nodded.

'Anything else?' I said.

He eyed me up down. 'What do you look like without that hat?'

I pulled the hat off and my blonde hair tumbled down to my shoulders. I'd washed and dried it that morning.

'Very pretty. Very sexy too.'

There was another awkward moment, and then he said, 'I'm having a party at my house tomorrow night. I'd like you to come along. Don't wear the hat. Don't tell anyone who you are. I'll handle that.'

'Why invite me?'

'Why not?'

'Because I don't belong in your world and you know that.'

'It's just a party, Phred.' He looked at me. 'Phred, what's that short for?'

'Nothing. That's my name.'

He lifted my mobile where I'd put it on the table and tapped a phone number into it.

'The party's at eight. Call if you can't find the address, though I'm sure the paparazzi know it better than I do.'

He pulled the collar of his coat up against the snow as he stepped outside the front door.

'See you tomorrow night.' He smiled, and looked more handsome than I'd ever seen him, standing there in the snowy night.

He walked away towards the limousine. A driver got out and opened the door for him, and then the car drove off.

I breathed in the icy air before going inside. Something felt different, a change in the watermark of how things were going to be.

I swiftly pushed these thoughts aside and got ready for the night ahead, when once again I would become part of the paparazzi.

Chapter Three

A Camera Full Of Gold Dust

The cold night air had an underlying feeling of excitement, as if the city was holding its breath, anticipating the night ahead. The snow created a whiteout, and every street, building and tree was iced white against the dark blue skyline. Everything was calm, waiting to come alive.

I'd agreed to do two assignments for the paper, but I'd explained to Royce that despite the money being very welcome, I didn't want to do this on a permanent basis. No more paparazzi stuff after tonight. It just wasn't for me.

I'd parked my car across the street from a hotel where a celebrity couple were ensconced. Royce wanted a photograph of them together to accompany an editorial about their impending engagement. All I had to do was sit in my car and wait for them to appear, and then dash over and snap a few pics. This seemed a lot easier than last night's fiasco at the premier.

I'd dressed for the weather in black cords, jumper, jacket, boots and hat. Everything was black, including my woolly hat. No colourful pom poms tonight. I planned to fade into the background, into the shadows, rather than attract attention.

Royce warned me that my photograph had been circulated around the paparazzi. Any anonymity I'd enjoyed was fleeting. They now knew who I was and what I looked like, though I could hardly have expected any less from the professional paps. So it was all the more necessary to keep a low profile. It was like having your face plastered on a wanted poster. I hoped none of them recognised my face tonight.

I tucked my hair inside the hat which had flaps to keep my ears warm, and checked that the camera was ready for action. I'd been practising with the camera, learning how to use the zoom lens, though I was taking no chances tonight. Everything was set to automatic. The camera should've been on the paper's payroll because it hardly needed me.

While I watched for any sign of the celebrities emerging from the hotel, I thought back to the things my friends in Dublin had said to me when I told them I was leaving Ireland.

'You must be mad! Giving up a good journalist's career in Dublin is crazy. What are you thinking? What about your job at the newspaper here? You'll never survive in New York. You barely survive in Dublin. Look at the mess you've made of things. No wonder your boyfriends leave in their droves.'

It was at this point I interrupted the sage advice being thrown down my throat, and explained that droves wasn't anywhere near being accurate. In fact, I'd say on the drove scale I was a minus two. I'd only had two serious relationships, and I don't mean the ones that were so fleeting or puerile they were a joke.

Finbar's betrayal had been the last straw. Was it any wonder I headed off to New York to make a fresh start.

Before I could screw myself into a pretzel thinking about the past, the celebrities appeared at the front door, in camera range. Unfortunately, several other paparazzi were after the same thing. Their shadows emerged from behind bins, cars and a darkened alley. I reckoned it was going to be a battle of the fastest and the fiercest.

Game on.

I hung the camera around my neck, got out of the car and scurried across the street.

The street was narrow, just off the main thoroughfare. The hard packed snow reflected the colourful lights of the hotel. Everything else was cast in shadow.

Two paparazzi lurked beside a tree. They'd blended so well into the landscape that I didn't see them until we were face to face.

I heard one of them say to the other, 'Look who's here.'

Two sets of disapproving eyes skewered me.

'Go home, girlie, you're out of your depths.'

He was probably right, but something in his tone really riled me. I blame the Irish fire in my blood.

So when the celebrities hurried from the hotel to their car, I put a spurt on, running like blazes to beat the other paparazzi. The snowy ground caused a few of the paps to slip and slide as they jostled with each other. My boots had ruts in the soles that gave a great grip. They were hill walking boots designed for rough terrain in all weather conditions, so I figured they'd be ideal for running with the paparazzi.

And I was right. I pipped the other paps at the post and got first dibs at the celebrity snaps. While I was running, I pressed my finger on the button and let the camera click off around twenty times in lightning fast succession.

Not only did I get several unobscured pictures of the couple, by some fluke, I got a close up of the woman's engagement ring as she got into the car. She'd put her hand up to shield her eyes from the flash of the cameras and I got a great shot of the diamond ring.

I ran back to my car, and having been well warned by Royce to get my priorities right, I downloaded the photographs on to my laptop. Four of them were winners, including the close up of the ring. If I could have danced inside my car I would have. I e–mailed them straight to Royce who was working on the paper's deadline at the office.

Ever on the alert, Royce confirmed within a couple of minutes that he'd got them, and asked me to write around five hundred words to go with the feature. I hadn't expected to have to write this, but I rattled it together, describing the couple, what they were wearing, how they looked together, and details of the ring which in the close up was a brilliant cut diamond set in yellow gold. Beautiful. In less than fifteen minutes, the pics and editorial were e–mailed off to Royce. Phew!

I drove off across the city to the next assignment. I had a busy night ahead of me, but there was the potential to earn more in one night than I had in the past month. Royce had kept his word about the money. A payment earned from the Bradley photograph had been paid into my bank account. I could breath easier about my next rent.

It was at this point that I wondered if I was being paranoid, but car headlights had followed me all the way across Manhattan. Was it the paparazzi on my tail? I doubted it. In the grand scheme of things I was a minor thorn in their sides. They were big boys. They could handle a little competition. Couldn't they?

Keeping an eye on my rear view mirror, I continued to the nightclub on the other side of the city. A huge celebrity event was taking place there. They were promoting the movie of a top rated television series, and numerous stars were attending. This assignment was a tricky one, and I wasn't sure whether or not I could pull it off.

Royce wanted candid shots of the main stars, not press release pics that every paper had been circulating in anticipation of the launch. I needed photographs of them arriving and leaving the nightclub. Nearly every pap in the city was going to be there. They knew the ropes far better than me.

I still didn't know what my tactics would be for this one as I drove up to the club. I parked as near as I could, but the street was jumping with cars, celebrities, fans and sheer mayhem. I was wondering if the zoom lens on my camera would pick up enough from the cocoon of my car, when I remembered about the car who'd been tailing me. I'd lost them at the last set of traffic lights. Now here they were, pulling up right behind me.

I kept the engine running and my wits about me.

The main beam of the headlights obscured the car. It was only when the beams dipped that I saw the silver limousine.

Bradley Goldsilver? What the heck was he doing following me? Not that I was complaining. Being followed by Bradley was many a woman's dream.

The limo door opened and out stepped Bradley, band box immaculate as usual in a stylish dark suit. He came right up to the car window and peered in at me.

'Good evening, Phred.'

I opened the window. 'Are you following me?'

'It would appear so.'

'How did you know where I was?'

'I got a tip–off. And it's a big event. I thought you'd be here. Most of the paparazzi are.'

I took the jab silently on the chin. He was right. Tonight I was officially one of the paparazzi.

'So what do you want with me?' I said.

He pressed those sensuous lips of his together thoughtfully. 'I'm not sure.'

'Well, while you're pondering this, you'll excuse me if I run because I'm missing some of the stars arriving.'

I opened the car door and he stepped back as I got out. Those gorgeous turquoise eyes looked at my outfit. 'Can you dance?'

'Dance? Yes, why?'

'You'd get better photographs if you were inside the nightclub rather than freezing out here.'

'Yes, but —'

'Take your jacket off and ditch the hat,' he said.

By now I'd noticed a couple of the paparazzi had seen Bradley and were heading this way. He'd seen them too. His expression urged me to do as he said.

I flung the jacket, chunky knit jumper and hat into the back seat, hung the camera round my neck, and locked the car. I was wearing a long sleeve, black thermal vest along with slim fitting black cords and the all terrain black boots.

Bradley nodded his approval.

I glanced at the paps. They were getting nearer. I heard them mention Bradley's name, and one of them thought I looked familiar.

'Run,' Bradley said, and grabbed my hand.

We ran towards the nightclub. I was smiling and panicking in the same breath. I'd never have dreamed that I'd be sprinting hand in hand with Mr mega movie star, along the snowy street, in the full glare of the paparazzi. I was on the wrong side of the cameras again.

Bradley's jacket flapped open as we ran, revealing his white shirt and tie. He looked great, blonde hair blowing back from his handsome face. What the hell was he doing with me?

'That's the pom pom chick,' one of the paps shouted.

I pulled my hand away from Bradley.

Several paparazzi cameras clicked in our direction.

We kept running.

I pretended to be chasing Bradley rather than get caught up in a scandal that we were somehow romantically involved with each other.

'Cute little blonde. Is he dating her?'

'No, she's press.'

Bradley and I arrived at the nightclub. Everyone knew who he was and the crowds of security men, media types and others in the industry, parted allowing us through and into the nightclub.

The scene was lively. Usually cameras, like the one around my neck, would not be allowed in. However, tonight was all about publicity and promotion and numerous media people had cameras.

The music was upbeat but not too loud, and the atmosphere was electric.

'Thank you, Phred,' said Bradley.

I knew what he meant. 'I didn't want anyone getting the wrong impression,' I said.

'I never thought I'd be thanking the paparazzi for saving me from scandal,' he said.

I smiled at him. Bradley had a sexy voice. Sometimes when he spoke I could hear the British tones in his accent, no doubt from his partial education in London.

'Bradley!' a woman said. She draped herself around him.

He peeled her off and we moved to another part of the club.

Inside the nightclub with its atmospheric lighting, my clothes didn't feel so out of place. My hair was tousled from wearing the woolly hat, running along the street with Bradley, and from harassment. I blended into the club scene, and it looked like I had a little bit of boho chic going on.

We stood near an alcove opposite the dance floor which was packed with people. Bradley was lit up by the neon spotlights while I merged into the shadows.

'Who are you supposed to pap tonight?' said Bradley.

'The main celebrities involved in the movie.'

Bradley hung my camera around his neck. 'Let's go.'

He led me over to a group of well known celebrities who were delighted to see him. He introduced me.

'This is Phred.'

'Hi. What do you do?' one of them asked.

'She's the paparazzi,' said Bradley.

They laughed.

'I'm learning her job.' Bradley flicked the camera on. 'Smile.'

Joining in on the joke, they posed and smiled for Bradley.

After chatting to them for a few minutes, we moved on, and he photographed other celebrities for me.

'There you are,' Bradley said to me. 'Now you can go home and get some sleep.'

'Your friends will go crazy when these come out in the press.'

'Nonsense. Everyone who's here tonight, apart from me, is here to see and be seen.

They're looking for publicity. That's how the game works, Phred.'

'I'd like a photograph of you with some of them,' I said.

Bradley gathered a group of his friends, all of them well known stars. 'How do you want us to pose?' he said, as they laughed and joined in the fun.

'Jump up in the air. Do something wild,' I said.

Without hesitation, they all jumped up, making poses and laughing heartily. I clicked a snap of them in perfect timing. I showed Bradley the preview. 'Brilliant. It's one for the archives,' he said, taking the camera back off me to save me from carrying it.

Then he led me on to the crowded dance floor. 'You said you could dance.' Bradley was a great dancer, even with the camera round his neck. It was the strangest night I'd had in a long time. But I enjoyed myself. I hadn't danced like this since I'd left Dublin. In New York my whole world had become working long hours at the newspaper.

The music changed, became even more upbeat, and we danced our socks off — Bradley the movie star and the wild Irish paparazzo.

Bradley finally phoned for the limo to be brought to the front door of the nightclub.

I wrapped my arms around myself to keep warm in the freezing night air outside the club. The street was busy with cars and paparazzi and lots of people coming and going, so we walked towards the limousine that was parked further along the street behind my car.

'What brought you to New York? Did something happen in Dublin?' he said.

'I got dumped by Finbar, my ex boyfriend, last November. I used that month's wages, which was everything I had, and headed to New York in December. Royce took me on to cover for his editorial staff who wanted time off at Christmas and New Year. After the holidays, Royce kept me on and I've worked there ever since.'

'What about your ex–boyfriend? Was he a journalist?'

'No, he owned a couple of bars in Dublin.'

'Do you miss him?'

'No, but I miss the thought of him.'

We reached the limo.

'I have to ask,' I said, 'but why is someone like you partying with a woman like me?'

He looked over at several female celebrities who were leaving the nightclub surrounded by their respective entourages. None of them were smiling or seemed to be having fun. It was all posturing, posing and barking orders at the men who were with them. Some of them could barely walk in the heels they were wearing and had to be helped into their cars. Bradley's expression said it all.

'You're great to talk to, Phred. I enjoyed myself tonight.'

'Me too.'

He gave me back the camera. 'Get some

sleep. And remember the party at my house.'

Then we went our separate ways.

I put my jumper and jacket on, turned up the heater in my car, and drove home with a camera full of gold dust.

'These are gold dust. How did you persuade them to pose like that?' Royce said next day when I showed him the celebrity photographs from the nightclub.

'Bradley photographed them.'

A moment's stunned silence, and in Royce's world it took a lot to flummox someone like him.

I gave him the short course of what had happened.

'You were dancing with Bradley Goldsilver?' I hadn't heard his voice so high since the helium balloon incident in the office last month during his birthday. I should never have dared him to hang upside down from the lintel of the door.

'Don't worry I won't be hitting the

headlines this time. The paparazzi didn't get any pictures of us. At least I don't think so.'

'No offence, Phred, but what is he doing hanging out with you? You almost fried his butt with that picture of him and Velvette.'

'He says I'm great to talk to. He seems to enjoy doing things that could get him into mischief.'

'Being friends a journalist like you would guarantee that. You're a magnet for trouble.'

'Thanks.'

'You know what I mean, Phred.'

I did. I really did.

Chapter Four

Skating On Thin Ice

'Bradley has invited me to a party he's having at his house tonight,' I said to Royce, letting the cat out of the bag.

'Are you going?'

'Let me see…sit at home alone watching a film on television or dress up and party with the rich and glamorous.'

'Take the camera with you.'

I went to protest, to tell him that this was play not work, but he insisted.

'Trust me on this, Phred. Take the camera.'

I sighed. 'Anything else I should do?'

'Yes. Don't let Bradley steal you,' Royce said.

'Steal me? That's ridiculous.'

'He's lining you up, kiddo. Trust me on that one too.'

The rest of the day was a blur of working on my usual general news and features for the paper — everything from the social scene and fashion features to being the motoring correspondent where I got to test drive cars. The next issue of the paper was heavy on the celebrity nightclub photographs, and there was a buzz in the office in anticipation that sales of the paper would skyrocket. This basically took the pressure off of everyone. Even though the dyed–in–the–wool reporters didn't rate the celebrity exclusives and would've preferred hard journalism to be increasing sales, what mattered was the bottom line. Our paper would shoot through the roof.

'Write a couple of pieces to go with these pics,' Royce said, putting several of the nightclub photographs down on my desk. 'You were there, describe the atmosphere. We'll run it over a few days, so give it legs. And add some captions. Coordinate those with the subs. They'll keep you right.'

I nodded.

'Oh and I know it was Bradley who took the pictures, but I'm crediting you on the byline and as the photographer. I've got to credit someone for the pics and it sure as hell isn't going to be him.'

'He knows we're going to run with these and he's okay with it. And there is one picture that's mine.' I pointed to the one of Bradley and the celebrities jumping up in the nightclub.

'My favourite,' Royce said, and then leaned down and spoke quietly. He was so close I could see the flecks of green in his blue eyes. 'Are you still going to his party tonight?'

'Yes.'

'I hear there's going to be plenty of A–listers as well as top producers and directors. A lot of networking will be going on. Keep your ears open. And don't be suckered into anything.'

'I won't.'

'Sure you will.' He handed me a piece of

paper. 'Here's Bradley's address. Take a cab. Don't be driving up in that shit heap of yours.'

'Don't diss the car. It's more reliable than yours or a few others in this office, even in icy conditions.'

'That's because you tinker with it.'

I laughed. 'At least I know how to change the spark plugs. You wouldn't know your crankshaft from your dipstick.'

'I know a dipstick when I see one, so watch your tail tonight with Bradley.'On that cheering thought, he left me to get on with my work.

But then there was a change of plan.

'I need to borrow Phred,' one of the advertising managers said to Royce. 'It's a rush job for a motoring ad–feat.'

Royce checked the time on his watch. 'As long as she's back by five. I'll need her then.'

'Sure thing,' he said.

'I don't have any photographers spare to go with you,' Royce said to me, 'so take a tripod.'

I grabbed my jacket, laptop, camera and a tripod that was in a corner of the office, and followed the ad manager who hurried outside to a brand new car parked in the street.

'With all this snow and lots more forecast, the car company want a big splash feature in the paper,' he explained at speed. 'I told them, if it's got wheels, Phred can drive it. They're emphasising the all–weather capabilities, heated seats, quick defrost, so test and highlight those sorts of things.' He handed me the keys and a brochure containing details of the specifications. 'Take it for a test drive.' He looked up at the sky. Snow was falling fast. 'And see if you can work the snow into the background when you're taking the pics, Phred.'

The car started first time from cold, and handled well in the snow through the city traffic. The heated seat kept my bum nice and toasty and it was the cosiest I'd felt in days. I liked the car. A lot. My editorial would confirm this.

For the photographs, I pulled up near Central Park and set up the camera on the tripod. The auto function clicked off five shots of the car with me sitting inside, looking out of the driver's side window. Usually a press photographer would take these, but the pictures turned out great against the city's wintry background.

The test drive and photographs went without a hitch, and as I drove back to the newspaper, I saw people skating on one of the outdoor rinks in the city centre. I was well ahead of schedule, and it looked so tempting. I'd always wanted to do this, but last December I was up to my eyeballs in work and the whole winter scene passed me by. I'd been determined that this winter I would enjoy New York, though so far all I'd done was work.

Somehow I talked myself into having a go. This would be the equivalent of my afternoon tea break. A sign advertised that skate hire and ten minutes on the rink was only a few dollars. Perfect.

I locked the car safely and went over to collect the skates. I ended up with a junior pair because my feet are quite small. This meant that the skate hire was half price or I could have twice the time on the rink. I opted to skate longer.

I tottered on to the rink, getting a feel for the ice. I hadn't skated in years, not since I was in my teens, but the technique soon came back to me. I'd never skated outdoors before and it was wonderful gliding over the ice with the cold, fresh air on my face and the snow falling gently all around. I'd worn my famous woolly pom pom hat to keep my ears warm. It was the only one I had with me, stuffed in the pocket of my jacket. I doubted anyone would recognise me. You didn't really get the paparazzi doing wobbly spins on the ice.

But there's always someone who sees you.

Before I knew it, a couple of guys were taking photographs of me. I didn't think they were paparazzi, more like photo–journalists. 'It's her. It's that paparazzi girl.'

Shit! I made a mad dash to the side of the rink where I deposited the skates with the hire guy.

'You've still got ten minutes skate time left,' he called to me as I hurried back to the car.

'Come on, start first time,' I urged the car. It did, and I drove off into the snow scene of traffic.

But I knew they'd got a couple of snaps of me. I glared at the hat in the mirror. It was time for some different hats.

I parked the car outside the newspaper building, and handed the keys back to the advertising manager who was delighted that the test drive was a success. I told him I'd write a motoring editorial and have the photographs with him before five.

I sent the finished feature to him by four–fifteen, and was working on other editorials at my desk when the figure of Royce loomed behind me. 'Is there no end to your talents?' he said sarcastically. He held up his phone which had a picture of me skating on thin ice.

Uh–oh, here we go, I thought, my heart sinking.

I traipsed after him into his office. It turned out that the two guys were indeed photo–journalists. They knew Royce. They recognised me and sent the pictures to him.

I sighed to myself. Ratted out again.

'I'm confiscating the hat,' Royce said.

I went through to get it, brought it back and put it on his desk in front of him. He opened a drawer, threw the hat inside, and shut the drawer again.

'Remember,' I said, 'these hats breed overnight.'

'The only thing breeding overnight is the trouble you're causing.'

I left him to it and got on with writing the captions for the celebrity features.

Before I knew it, the work was finished, and it was time to head home and get ready for the party.

There really was nothing wrong with my car. The paintwork had seen better days, but it could pass okay, and the engine had a very reassuring growl. It was a decent secondhand car that was just fine. If it had been embarrassingly awful I would've taken a cab. But it wasn't. So I didn't.

I had the heater turned up full. The oyster satin evening dress I'd chosen to wear provided very little warmth. I wore a fluffy white bolero to keep my shoulders cosy, and sparkly high heeled shoes. The dress was the only full length one I had. I'd picked it up at a bargain vintage shop months ago and never worn it. I liked it because it was a simple figure skimming sheath dress with shoe string straps. The oyster satin suited my pale skin, green eyes, and blonde colouring, and reminded me of dresses from the classic 1930s era. I'd kept my hair down, sleek and smooth, and make up to a minimum — gold eye make up, mascara, and rose coloured lip gloss. No jewellery, no fuss, and a little sequin clutch bag.

Bradley's house, a white stone mansion in an upmarket area of Manhattan, was all lit up and alive with cars arriving. The driveway was cleared of snow, as was the parking area. It was snowing as I arrived which added to the magical feel of the evening. I might never be at a party like this again, and I was committing everything to memory. I parked my car beside the other limousines and expensive saloons. No one gave it a second glance. They were too busy heading into the party, and because it was snowing, all the cars were sprinkled white and blended into the scenery.

I'd taken Royce's advice and had the camera in the boot of the car. I left it there, and my laptop, and walked towards the house, wondering what sort of night was in store. A glamorous one that's for sure, judging by some of the outlandish outfits the guests were wearing. Then it dawned on me — most of them were wearing fancy dress. Bradley never mentioned anything about wearing a costume.

Was this part of the set up that Royce had warned me of? Was Bradley trying to make me stand out from the crowd for not wearing an outfit? Surely not. I was already the outsider.

I paused, thinking what to do. Giving up and going back home defeated wasn't my style. And I had been looking forward to the party.

The large front door was open, the expanse of windows all aglow, and inside I could see a whole world of excitement, dancing and glamour. There it was — the other life that I'd seen in films and magazines, and that I'd written about in the press. Tonight I had a chance to be part of it.

Chapter Five

Cake In November

Guests were vetted as they arrived to ensure there were no party crashers. I was approached by one of the beautiful, statuesque hostesses at the door. She looked down her nose at me, and I could sense that the welcome mat was about to be ripped out from under me.

'This is a fancy dress party. Where's your costume?' she said. 'Who invited you anyway?'

'Bradley.'

She sneered at me in disbelief. 'Really?'

'Yes, really.'

'No costume, no party,' she took great pleasure in telling me.

I turned to leave.

'Wait, Phred. I forgot to mention about the fancy dress but it doesn't matter.' Bradley hurried to welcome me in. He was dressed as a 1920s gangster.

The hostess glared at me with undiluted vitriol.

I smiled at Bradley. 'No, I have my outfit in the car. I'll go get it.'

I went back out into the cold, fetched my camera from the car, and hung it around my neck.

'What are you supposed to be?' the woman said, wrinkling her nose in disdain when I came back.

I smiled and clicked a snap of her.

'I'm the paparazzi.'

Bradley laughed. 'Come on, have a drink,' he said, sweeping me away to the heart of the party. En route he had a word in the ear of one of the security staff to tell the snippy hostess to go home because her services were no longer required.

I opted for a soft drink.

'Oh come on, have some champagne,' said Bradley.

'I'm driving,' I said, which was true, but it was also an excuse to keep a clear head.

Royce's warnings were replaying in my thoughts. I'd already been thankful that I'd taken his advice and brought the camera with me.

Bradley held a glass of champagne and said a little too loud, 'You don't have to drive home. You can sleep here tonight.'

Amid the noise of the party his words caused a lull as everyone around us stared to see who Bradley was propositioning.

He laughed again and pulled me away from them.

'You're completely wicked,' I said.

'Wicked? I've never been called that before. But I quite like the sound of it. I was of course meaning you could sleepover in one of the numerous spare bedrooms.' He was smiling, I could feel the stress lift from my shoulders and I actually began to laugh along with him.

'Let's both be wicked,' he said. 'There's someone I'd like you to meet. He completely disapproves of me being friends with you. He thinks you'll be nothing but trouble.'

'Why?' I said, remembering Royce had told me I'd be a magnet for trouble.

'Because you're the paparazzi. He doesn't trust them. He thinks you'll have hidden cameras on you, perhaps in a brooch or a button, and then the photographs will be splashed across the newspapers as headline gossip. I told him that you're a reluctant paparazzi but he's still suspicious.'

'He sounds like a bundle of laughs,' I said.

'I have my moments,' a man's voice said behind us.

'Ah, there you are, Vaughn,' said Bradley. 'I'd like you to meet Phred.'

He shook hands with me. 'Miss O'Leary.'

I wasn't sure what to say because I was thinking how handsome he was. In contrast to Bradley's blonde hair, he had rich, dark hair and pale grey eyes. Similar in height, age and build to Bradley, and just as immaculate in a black dinner suit, I assumed he was a movie star.

'Vaughn's my agent,' Bradley said, shattering my assumptions. 'He's one of the top in the industry.'

I realised I was still holding Vaughn's hand, or perhaps he was holding mine. I let go.

'What did you come as?' Bradley asked Vaughn.

Vaughn pulled a fake gun from his jacket pocket. 'I'm a *secret* agent.'

'Excellent,' said Bradley.

A snowman trundled past. 'Thawed out, he's the producer of my next movie,' said Bradley.

The snowman gave us a nod and toddled on.

'Have you read over the new script?' Vaughn asked Bradley.

'Yes . . .'

'What do you think of it?' said Vaughn.

Bradley sighed. 'It's lacking any real depth. It could do with a rewrite.'

Vaughn nodded.

Bradley looked at me. 'Have you done any script doctoring?'

'Eh, a little bit, mainly for stage plays back in Ireland. And one full length screenplay.'

'I'd like you to read over the script. It's science fiction, lots of action. See what you can do with it,' said Bradley.

I agreed, thinking it was more of a favour, which I was happy to do.

'How long will it take you?' Bradley said, sounding as if it was urgent.

I glanced at the time. The evening was young. 'Hmm, about four hours.'

Bradley's eyes widened.

'Okay, how about three hours,' I said, thinking he wanted me to work faster.

Vaughn burst out laughing.

My heart started to race as I wondered if I could somehow do it quicker. Working at the newspaper office I was used to meeting crushing deadlines. After a while, writing everything at speed became natural. I got used to the pace of it. There was no time to dwell on it, and no place for excuses. As a journalist, if I didn't have an editorial ready when Royce was waiting for it, this could cause chaos for the paper. Basically this couldn't happen. I had to meet the deadlines, every one of them, or I was out of the game. It was that simple.

Bradley smiled at me. 'Three hours? I was thinking three days or even three weeks.'

'Well, if you're looking for a total rewrite then yes, three days or more, but to give it the once over, crisp up the dialogue, then I can have it done by the end of the night.'

Bradley was all fired up with enthusiasm. 'What would you need?'

'My laptop and somewhere quiet. No interruptions and let me get on with it.''You'd really give up the party to work on the script?' said Vaughn.

'Yes, I'm more used to working than I am to partying.'

'Somewhere quiet?' Bradley mused.

'That would be my house,' said Vaughn.

‘Exactly,’ said Bradley. ‘Vaughn’s house is a haven of calm and genteel behaviour.’

And so I ended up at Vaughn’s house.

We drove there in minutes in Vaughn’s car, a luxury saloon that smelled of expensive leather and money. There were no sticky finger marks or signs that kids had ever set foot in it, and I noticed he wasn’t wearing a wedding ring. The fact that I was trying to figure out if Vaughn was single or married with kids, bothered me. What was I thinking? I put my errant thoughts down to the recent craziness, which was about to include upgrading a movie script in the house of one of the main movers and shakers in the film industry. I could’ve been home baking cakes, or out running with the paparazzi. How strange my life had become.

I liked Vaughn’s house as soon as I saw it. It was a traditional mansion rather than the modern style of Bradley’s. Lots of trees protected the property from prying eyes, again unlike Bradley’s whose house was open to view.

I liked it even more once I stepped inside. It was old money, classy, rich woods, burgundy, golds, deep pile carpets and sumptuous sofas. Table lamps gave a warm glow to the lounge, and Vaughn lit the fire that was set in the fireplace. The house was already mildly warm, though perhaps it was my temperature rising every time Vaughn came near me.

Vaughn's voice was as rich and deep as his surroundings.

'Will this suit you? Can you work in here?'

'This is ideal.'

'My office is through there. Give me your e–mail and I'll send you a copy of the script.'

He sent the script in minutes, and came back with a pot of coffee and biscuits which he put down on a table near the fire. 'Call if you need anything.'

And then he left me to get on with the writing.

I opened the e–mail on my laptop and read the script's page count. One hundred and twenty pages. I could do this. I could.

I poured myself a cup of coffee and started work on the script. I put all thoughts of Vaughn out of my mind and concentrated on the writing. Nothing else.

Three hours later I was finished.

'You may not agree with what I've done with it, but there was a major flaw in the storyline. I changed it around which sorted out quite a few other problems, and I sharpened up the dialogue.'

Vaughn's pale grey eyes studied the first few pages of the script on my laptop. He leaned close, not intentionally making my heart race, but that's the effect he had on me.

'This is great, Phred. A first–class job. I can't thank you enough.'

'You're welcome.'

He looked at me and smiled, and for a moment, I thought he saw me in a different light. Not the journalist or the paparazzi or the magnet for trouble, but the way a man looks at a woman — that spark, that indefinable something.

'Shall we go?' he said.

I closed my laptop. 'Yes.'

Flurries of snow swirled around me when Vaughn opened the front door.

His car was parked in the driveway and he shielded me with his body, wrapping his arms around me while I held tight to the laptop and made a dash for the car. He opened the passenger door and I jumped in. Vaughn ran round and got into the driver's side. He shook the snow from his hair.

'You'll be able to build a snowman,' I said, looking out the window at his garden which was covered in a thick layer of snow.

The comment was out before I could stop it, and I'm sure it made me sound really childish, but I loved the snow and half the fun was being able to build a snowman.

'I don't think I've ever built one,' he said, starting up the car, turning the heater up, and driving off.

'You must think I'm silly,' I said.

'Not at all. I think you're very natural. I find that refreshing — and so does Bradley. I can see why he likes you.'

I blushed.

'You seem to like him,' he said.

'I do. Bradley's great.'

'He is. I'm his agent, but we've been friends for years.'

We arrived back at Bradley's house where the party was in full flow. He couldn't wait to see what I'd done with the script. We went through to his office that was all cream and white, and I e–mailed it to his laptop.

'Phred's worked her magic on the script,' said Vaughn. 'From what I've read so far, I think you'll like it.'

Bradley was already lost in reading the script. We left him to it and went to get something to eat at the buffet.

Heading to the buffet, I noticed that many of the women at the party were beautiful, some of the top models, celebrities and movie stars. I could never hope to compete, and I honestly didn't want to. Being high maintenance was never one of my ambitions.

'Are you hungry?' said Vaughn.

'Starving. I missed breakfast, lunch was a blur, and didn't have time to cook dinner before coming here.'

'Well, make sure you have something to eat now,' he said, helping me select from the delicious buffet. I thought his manners were impeccable.

'Would you like anything else?' he said.

'Can I have a slice of cake too, please?' I said.

'Yes, which one?'

'The one with the white icing. It looks like birthday cake.'

'Is it your birthday?'

'I don't know.'

'You don't know?'

'It's definitely one day in November.'

Vaughn frowned. 'Why don't you know what date your birthday is?'

'I was abandoned when I was a baby, so I

was brought up by the authorities. The only thing I know for sure is my name and that I was born in November.' I wasn't looking for sympathy, just cake.

'I'm sorry,' he said. 'Why don't you choose a date in November?'

'Because it could be the wrong date, and then I'd never celebrate the real day. So I have some sort of cake each day in November. Yesterday I had an iced doughnut. The day before that a cupcake. And I bake my own cakes when I have the time. It's become like a tradition, but I've been so busy I haven't had time to have any cake today.'

'I've never met anyone like you,' he said.

I smiled, and we sat down to enjoy our food when the snowman (producer) waved Vaughn to come over.

'Excuse me,' Vaughn said. 'I'll be back in a minute.'

I heard the snowman say to Vaughn, 'She rewrote the script? This evening? If she can upgrade at that rate, I'm hiring her.'

‘I’ll keep that in mind,’ said Vaughn.

‘Do that. Seriously. I have several projects where the scripts need doctored. I assume you’re handling her?’

‘Yes,’ said Vaughn.

I almost choked on my salad. Now I had an agent? Though maybe Vaughn was saying this to appease the producer? I couldn’t possibly be on Vaughn’s exclusive list of clients. Could I?

‘Set up a meeting. I’d like to talk to her when I’m not dressed as a snowman,’ the producer said.

Vaughn nodded, and the snowman trundled off again.

When Vaughn came back I pretended I hadn’t heard anything.

Bradley bounded over to us and sat beside me on the sofa. ‘I love it! I love what you’ve done with the script. Sorting that part of the storyline has made a world of difference to my character. I’ve had a quick skim of the script, but it’s great. I’ll read every bit of it tonight after the party.'

'I'm pleased you like it,' I said.

He handed me a cheque. 'This is for you.'

I gasped when I saw the amount. 'Ten thousand dollars?' I gave it back to him. 'No, no, I can't take this.'

'Why not? You've earned it.'

'I didn't think I was working for you. I only did it because…I thought we were becoming friends.'

Bradley and Vaughn were stunned.

'You did this out of *friendship*?' Bradley said, sounding as if this was a completely alien concept.

'Yes. I wasn't looking for any money. I did it to help you. I thought you needed it.'

Bradley glanced at Vaughn, who registered the same level of disbelief.

Bradley's eyes welled up. 'That's the nicest thing anyone's done for me in a long time.' And then he gave me a huge hug. When he finally let go of me he added, 'We are friends, Phred. You and me, we're definitely friends.'

We smiled at each other.

He pressed the cheque back into my hands. 'But, as your friend, I really want you to take this, okay? It's for your time and expertise. If the script is used in production, you'll be paid a further amount and be credited as one of the writers.'

I was still reluctant. The money was great, but I've never liked taking payment for something that I thought was done freely.

'Listen,' said Bradley. 'I want you to take it. The money will come out of the movie budget anyway.'

Vaughn nodded. And Bradley put the cheque in my evening bag.

'Thank you,' I said.

'Right,' said Bradley, 'Let's dance.' He went to pull me up but Vaughn intervened.

'Not until she's had her birthday cake,' said Vaughn, smiling.

'It's your birthday, Phred?' Bradley said,

his face lighting up with enthusiasm.

'Maybe,' I said.

Vaughn explained about me eating cake every day in November.

Bradley thought this was brilliant. 'You gotta love her,' he said to Vaughn.

Vaughn gave me a smile that almost made me melt. 'Definitely,' he said, gazing right at me with those stunning grey eyes.

So we all had cake and enjoyed the party. I danced with Bradley, and then as the music slowed, Vaughn cut in.

Bradley went off to dance with a woman who was slated to co–star with him in his next movie. There were already hints of a romance. Velvette was now part of his past.

'There's a producer who'd like to meet you, Phred,' said Vaughn.

I felt comfortable in his arms as we slow danced, as if I fitted into him.

'He wants me to set up a meeting. Are you up for that?'

'Is this about the scriptwriting?' I said,

knowing it was.

'Yes, he's got several scripts that he'd like you to rewrite.'

My mind was ticking over the possibilities.

'You'd be extremely well paid. I'd handle the contracts for you.'

I knew how agents worked. Vaughn would get a cut of my fee.

He must have read my thoughts. 'I won't be taking any payment. The money will be all yours.'

All I could say was, 'Why?' I mean, what was the catch?

'I don't need the money. It'll kick start you into the industry. What do you say, Phred?'

'Pinch me, I'm dreaming?'

He laughed.

'But I'm working for Royce. I don't know that I'd risk walking away from the newspaper on the strength of rewriting the scripts. Perhaps I could do both, to begin with, until I find some security?'

'Very wise, and I'd advise you to do that.'

'It's becoming a blizzard out there,' someone said. People were hurrying to leave the party.

'I think I'd better go before it gets any heavier,' I said.

'You can't drive home in this,' Bradley said, suddenly back beside us again.

'My car can handle it.'

I put my bolero on, picked up my laptop, thanked Bradley, and hurried outside. But then I felt Vaughn lift me up and carry me to my car. As I wasn't dressed for a snow storm, I was grateful for his chivalry. Vaughn felt strong, very strong, with lean muscles under his suit. He shielded me as I got into the car.

'Drive safe.'

I nodded, started up the car, flicked the headlights on and cleared the snow from the front and rear windscreens with the wipers. The heater churned out warmth, and I drove off, blending into the stream of other cars leaving the party. I saw the solitary figure of Bradley standing on the first floor balcony watching people leave. Of course, a number of guests stayed overnight.

I arrived home, my thoughts rewinding the events of the evening. The apartment was cold, but the cheque was burning a hole in my bag. I flicked the heating on, turning it up for extra warmth, knowing I could afford to do this.

I hung up my dress, washed my make up off, made myself a cup of tea, and took the laptop with me to bed. Sitting cosy under the duvet, I searched the Internet for information about Vaughn and Bradley.

Vaughn was single, no messy entanglements with women, no children. He was from money, brought up in Hollywood, parents were investors/movie producers. Vaughn had acquired some of the top actors and writers in the business along with a lot of respect. He had more money than Bradley who was one of the leading A–listers. Vaughn had a reputation for being a serious natured businessman. On the flip side, he was considered to be quite a catch and totally luscious. I had no way to confirm the former but I agreed with the latter. Bradley was known as a wil–l–o'–the–wisp who threw great parties and had numerous entanglements with women. He'd made a string of science fiction action movies, all of them box office successes, though he'd never been nominated for any acting awards. If even some of this was true, Bradley was what I thought he was, and Vaughn was what I hoped he'd be. Not that I had a snowball's chance of dating Vaughn, but a girl can dream can't she?

Watching the snow falling outside my window, I snuggled down under the duvet to get some sleep. I don't know why, but I suddenly felt a long way from home, from Dublin. Would I ever go back? I wasn't sure. In fact, I wasn't sure about anything. I felt as if everything was going to change, and nothing would ever be the same again.

Chapter Six

Building A Snowman

'You've got an agent now?' Royce said. 'Vaughn is one of the top agents in the business. Doesn't he represent Bradley?'

'Yes, that's how we met, at the party last night.'

We were in his office. I didn't tell him I'd rewritten the script or about the ten thousand dollars. He wasn't interested anyway.

He glanced at my white fluffy hat that I'd worn this morning to look different but made no comment.

'Did you take the camera with you?'

'Yes, but —'

'What pictures have you got for me?'

'No pictures. I was a guest at the party.'

He shook his head. 'And what the hell do you need an agent for?'

'For my scriptwriting.'

He shook his head again and sneered. 'Everyone's got a script they're trying to sell. You haven't a hope in hell. Not even if you flash your tits at them.'

'Well, isn't that just grand.'

He handed me four assignments. 'Work on these today, and I'll have some more for you tonight.'

'This is paparazzi work. Why do you need me to do these? Your paps can handle them.'

'I want you to do it.'

'I told you I wasn't doing any more paparazzi stuff. What about my regular editorials and features?'

'I've farmed them out to the other reporters — for the foreseeable future.'

'So you're giving me no choice. If I don't do the paparazzi work, you don't have any other work for me.'

'It doesn't have to be like this, Phred. You're great at the paparazzi work.'

'I'm twenty–eight years old. I don't want

to be starting out as a paparazzo.'

'Take the assignments or there's nothing else for you.'

Any icy shiver ran through me. He wasn't bluffing. Royce never bluffed. He was betting I'd crumble and he'd have me working as one of the paparazzi.

'You'd really let me go?' I said.

'It's your choice.'

One of the subs called Royce through to the main office.

While several of them discussed the paper's layout and argued over the lead story, I packed the few items I owned into my bag, put the camera on the desk, and left without any of them noticing I'd gone.

I drove through Manhattan and stopped at Central Park. I got out and walked in the snow, breathing in the freezing cold air, trying to quell the waves of panic that were threatening to engulf me. What had I done? Was it too late to turn back? Royce and the others would never know I'd left if I went back now. I glanced across the city in the direction of the newspaper office. I stopped and stood right on the brink of decision. Should I give in and take the paparazzi work? Or did I have the guts to make the jump to the scriptwriting? No matter how tempted I was to take the safe route, I just couldn't go back to the newspaper. It was over. Truly over.

I blinked back the tears, turned my back on the paper, and went for a walk in the snow. Royce didn't phone me, which was a real stab to the heart. I think deep down he was jealous of my friendship with Bradley. There were other newspapers in the city, though I'd learned from hard experience from when I'd first arrived in the city that newspaper jobs were difficult to find. Freelance work would be my only route, and even those gaps were fiercely fought for.

After an hour, I headed home.

Vaughn was the first to phone me. 'Are you available to go to a meeting with the producer tomorrow afternoon at three?'

'Yes. Where do I have to go? And what do I need to take with me?'

'I'll e–mail the address to you, or I can pick you up and take you there. Bring samples of your work, any scripts you've written.'

'Okay, thanks Vaughn.'

He was quiet for a moment then he said, 'Has something happened?'

I sighed and tried to keep my voice steady. 'Royce just backed me into a corner. I can either work as one of the paparazzi for the paper or there's no other work available for me. He's given all my usual editorial and feature work to the other reporters. So I've left, and I'm not going back.'

'Where are you?'

'At home.'

'Drive to my house. Or do you want me to come and get you?'

'No, I'm on my way.'

I found Vaughn's house easily enough as it

wasn't far from Bradley's house whose address was fresh in my memory.

The sky was grey and the house seemed welcoming. The lights were on inside and the front door was open.

Vaughn came out to meet me. He was wearing a chunky cream sweater, and although casually dressed, he still looked like money. A blue scarf was tied around his neck and he had black gloves on.

'So, are you going to show me how to make a snowman?' he said, instead of taking me inside where I'd no doubt moan about being hard done to by Royce.

'We'll start with the body,' I said, taking my gloves from my jacket pocket and putting them on.

I gathered a ball of snow and showed him how to roll it to make it bigger.

'Got it,' he said, and while he made the body, I made the head. And we talked...about everything and nothing...and I felt better by the time our snowman was finished.

We set him up in the front lawn so we could see him from the window of the lounge. And after a snowball fight, which Vaughn lost, badly, we went inside to get a heat by the fire and drank mugs of hot chocolate that I'd made for us in his enviable, well stocked kitchen. I loved the kitchen. It was all browns, copper, gleaming black and rich wood. Vaughn said he dined out most of the time and hardly used the kitchen except to make coffee and snacks. He had people who tended the house for him but they didn't live in. He liked his privacy.

'I haven't had hot chocolate like this since I was a kid,' Vaughn said, smiling at the generous amount of marshmallows floating in his mug.

'You've learned to build a snowman and now you're drinking hot chocolate. I think I could be a bad influence on you.'

'A very bad influence. Don't forget the snowball fight.'

'You need to practise your technique. You throw like a girl.' I was teasing him of course.

'Not like a girl I know who threw snowballs at me without mercy.'

'It's the only way to learn.'

He laughed, and then he said, 'What type of cake did you have today?'

'I haven't had any.'

Vaughn stood up. 'We'll have to do something about that.' He went off to the kitchen and I followed him. 'No cake,' he said, searching the cupboards. 'Plenty of cookies but no cake.'

'Never mind,' I said.

Vaughn's phone rang. It was Bradley. 'She's here with me,' said Vaughn. 'Party? Yes, we'll be there. Do you have cake? Yes, for Phred's birthday. Great. See you later.' He rang off and said to me, 'Bradley's having a party tonight. You're invited.'

'Another party?'

'Don't you want to go? There are people you should meet.'

I did want to go to the party, especially

with the day I'd had. There was only one problem. 'Is it fancy dress?'

'No, just the usual evening dress. I'll drive you home and you can pick up a dress.'

I hesitated. 'I've only got one dress. And I wore it last night.'

Vaughn's expression changed. I could see he felt sorry for me.

I offered to drive downtown and buy one, but he said that due to the heavy snow, I could get caught up in the city centre's traffic. He had another idea. He phoned Bradley. 'Phred needs a dress for tonight. Do you have anything? Thanks.' He rang off again.

'Bradley's sending some over.'

'He has dresses?'

'Bradley has everything. He collects costumes from the movie sets.'

'So I could be dressing up as a sci–fi alien?'

'It's a distinct possibility.'

I laughed. 'And I thought my world was crazy.'

Bradley had someone send round a selection of dresses he thought would fit me.'These dresses are beautiful,' I said, admiring each one.

I chose a sparkly blue dress that glittered in the light. The design was sleek and the material was stunning.

'Try it on. Try them all on if you want,' said Vaughn.

I did. Some of them twice. I disappeared into one of Vaughn's spare bedrooms, laid the clothes on the huge, sumptuous bed, and got totally lost in the movie style dresses.

I already had a pair of high heeled shoes. I always kept a change of clothing and at least one pair of dry boots and shoes with me in the car. I often got soaked going out and about doing the journalism, and I liked to have something to change into. And with clearing out my desk at the office, I also had a few extra items in the car, including make up.

'How's it going in there?' Vaughn said, finally coming to rescue me from the clutches of silk and sparkle.

I opened the bedroom door. 'What do you think?' I said, giving him a twirl of the sparkly blue dress I was wearing.

'I think you're lovely, Phred. I don't think you realise how lovely you are.'

I laughed off his compliments, feeling slightly embarrassed.

'Shall we go?' he said.

It was time to go? Already?

'You've been in here for three hours,' he said, checking his watch.

I gasped. 'Three hours?'

He burst out laughing. 'No, just kidding. An hour. There had to be payback for beating me with the snowballs.'

And so, in a happy mood, I fixed my hair and make up, and we headed to Bradley's house. In all the fun I'd had with Vaughn, it had taken the edge off the fact that I'd left the newspaper. I was sure it would hit me later when I was home in bed, but for now, I didn't dwell on it.

‘Does Bradley have parties every night?’ I said to Vaughn.

‘No, but he has a lot of parties when one of his new movies comes out. It’s all part of the launch and publicity process. Then he quietens down again.’ He gave me a wry smile. ‘Sort of.’

Bradley’s house was ablaze of excitement and activity. It was even busier than the previous night. Within the cream and white decor, a couple of bars were set up, a buffet, and a dance floor that was already filled with couples dancing.

Bradley had a birthday cake for me, a proper one with candles. I blew them out and made a wish.

Vaughn introduced me to several movers and shakers in the film industry he thought I should meet. Vaughn, Bradley and I were chatting to them when one of the security men gave Bradley a business card. ‘A newspaper editor wants to talk to you. He’s outside at the front door. He says it’s personal. He wants two minutes of your time.'

Bradley read the name on the card as if it was poison. 'Royce.'

'I'll talk to him,' I said, not wanting any trouble.

'He wants to talk to Bradley. He made that quite clear,' the security man said.

The amenable party happy Bradley changed before my eyes into a darker version of himself. 'No, Phred, I'll handle Royce. I won't be long.'

I heard the security man murmur, 'Shit.' Those who knew Bradley seemed confident who their money was on and it wasn't the New York editor.

I was lurking at the door eavesdropping, and Vaughn was on standby to keep me in check. I peeked out the window. Royce stood outside in the snow, wearing a dark coat with the collar turned up.

Bradley went straight for Royce. 'Have you come to offer Phred her job back?'

Royce didn't flinch. 'No. The offer of the

paparazzi work I made this morning still stands. I didn't come here to compromise, or talk to her, though I assume she's here.'

Bradley didn't confirm or deny it.

'What did you want to say to me?' Bradley said.

Royce took one step closer, matching Bradley in height.

'You'd better treat her right,' Royce said.

'Better than you,' said Bradley. 'At least she won't be struggling to pay her next month's rent and economising on her heating when it's freezing cold in her apartment.'

Royce reacted as if he'd been verbally slapped in the face.

Bradley kept the pressure on. 'What? You never thought about it, did you, Royce?'

Royce didn't reply.

'No, I didn't think so,' said Bradley.

Royce's voice was deep with suspicion. 'I don't know what the hell you're up to with her.'

'I like her. I like Phred. It's not

complicated. If more women were like her, I wouldn't be such a . . . what is it you and your paper insinuated I was? Oh yes, a philandering dick–head.'

Royce turned and walked away, and said over his shoulder. 'Tell Phred I'm sorry it was such a harsh goodbye.'

Bradley shouted after him, 'I would, if I thought it was true.'

Royce didn't look back. He trudged to his car, got in and drove off.

Bradley and I didn't discuss what had happened. He simply put his arm around my shoulders, gave me a reassuring smile, and the three of us went back into the party.

I had another slice of cake, and everything was fine, until the fight started.

Chapter Seven

It's A Blizzard Out There

'She's the paparazzi.'

An actor from the movie premier during the pom pom fiasco recognised me.

Vaughn and I were dancing. He held me close and whispered in my ear, 'Ignore him. He's drunk.'

I ignored him. Basically, everyone ignored him.

Determined not to be ignored, the actor repeated his warning, louder and with more emphasis. 'She's the fuckin' paparazzi.'

Well that got everyone's attention.

It was one thing for Bradley to introduce me to his friends as the paparazzi, because they really never believed him, but it was quite another thing for this actor to point the finger at me.

As most of the celebrities were letting

their hair down, in the relative privacy of Bradley's house, news that the paparazzi were at the party caused chaos, and some of them started squabbling.

'I thought she was a scriptwriter,' a director snapped at Vaughn.

'She is.'

'Phred's no longer working for the press,' Bradley announced.

As if to make Bradley out to be a liar, another man pointed at me. 'I recognise you. I saw you in the paper today test driving a car in the snow.'

'That was the last feature I wrote before I left the newspaper,' I said. The feature had come out well, and with the car company paying for extra space in the paper, the photograph of me sitting in the car was quite big. You could see my face quite clearly, though I hadn't thought anyone here would recognise me.

A few curled lips showed their disbelief.

With emotions running high, and lots of

alcohol consumed, the situation flared up. I don't know who threw the first punch, but Vaughn became the target of the disgruntled actor's wrath, and when I saw that Vaughn was in danger of being punched in the face, I stepped in to help him.

When I say I stepped in, I mean I literally blocked the guy's attack and sent him reeling. I used minimum force, just enough to stop him punching Vaughn and possibly breaking his nose. But the way the actor flew through the air and landed near the buffet added spectacle and drama.

Everyone was rather surprised. Vaughn hadn't seen that one coming — the punch or my reaction to it.

'Wowza! Did you see the speed of that?' one man said.

Bradley was the first to laugh, and gave me a round of applause. Others joined in, clapping and smiling, and the fiery atmosphere fizzled out like a damp squib.

All issues with me being the paparazzi

were brushed aside in favour of my fighting ability and madcap motoring.

The director who had snapped at Vaughn changed his tune. 'I'm sorry, Vaughn. I was out of line. Set up a meeting. Your young lady could be very useful.'

How could I be useful as a writer because I could fight?

The troublemaker (who wasn't me) was escorted out by a couple of the security staff. Bradley assured me there would be no backlash to deal with. 'He's always causing fights when he's drunk and then apologising when he's sober.' He smiled at me. 'Nice moves though, Phred.'

'Where did you learn to fight like that?' said Vaughn.

'Sixteen years of martial arts in Dublin since I was a kid. Karate mainly,' I said.

'Any other lethal or hidden talents we should be aware of?' said Bradley.

'No, that's about it.'

'You sure?' said Vaughn.

'I enjoy painting and dressmaking, but I doubt my watercolours or a bodkin will cause you any harm.'

'It's a blizzard out there,' someone shouted.

I looked out the window, and all I could see was thick snow falling fast.

People started leaving.

Vaughn put his jacket on me and held me tight as we stepped outside and made a dash for his car. The strong wind was biting cold. I was freezing. Ball gowns and blizzards just didn't go well together, unlike Vaughn and me.

I pulled his jacket around me for warmth as he drove us back to his house with the intention of picking up my ordinary clothes and laptop, leaving the Cinderella glitz, and driving back home to my apartment before the weather became worse and I was snowed in. I glanced over at him as he concentrated on driving us safely. Visibility was bad, but he handled the car well. His crisp white shirt emphasised his broad shoulders and lean torso, and I wondered what he did to keep in shape, or whether he was one of those men who was naturally strong and hunky.

'Do you train to keep in shape?' I said.

'No, I just keep busy.'

Within minutes we arrived at his house. My car was parked in the driveway. It was covered in snow. He lifted me from the car and carried me over the snowy ground, depositing me inside the hallway.

We looked outside at the blizzard.

'Safer to stay here tonight,' he said.

'I could make it if I left right now.'

'No, the weather's getting worse. And besides, you'd need to be back here in the morning. We have to go over our strategy for the meeting tomorrow afternoon.'

This was true. And there were worse things than a sleepover at Vaughn's mansion.

I changed out of my evening dress and high heels into my black cords, warm socks, and a cosy red jumper that belonged to Vaughn.

I made us tea (for me) and coffee while Vaughn lit the fire in the lounge. I sat on the sofa with my laptop, while he relaxed on a chair beside the fire with his laptop. He'd had a phone call from the producer (snowman) while I was making tea. The producer had e–mailed information about the meeting, and about the script I'd rewritten for Bradley. The producer had also e–mailed Vaughn five scripts. He wanted to see if any of these would be something I could work with, and was giving me a chance to read them overnight ready for the meeting next day. This suited me. I wanted to be prepared. I wasn't a complete novice, but I'd never been in this league before.

Vaughn read the e–mail, and then he said, 'They're going to pay you extra because the producer liked what you did with Bradley's script. It's been approved. They're going ahead with the change in storyline. You'll be credited as one of the scriptwriters.'

My face lit up with excitement.

'Credits are valuable,' he said. 'They're like currency in this business. You'll get more offers once this ball starts rolling. But fair warning. You'll have to prove your worth, and work damn hard.'

'That's fine with me.'

'In the morning we'll go over the plan for the meeting. I'll tell you what you have to say.'

'Can't I just talk normal?'

'The producer is a hard businessman. He's a very successful producer and property owner with houses all over the city. The bottom line with him is money.'

'It's the same in the newspaper business.'

'True, but you can't just speak your mind at this meeting, Phred.'

'I'll be tactful. Truthful but tactful.'

Vaughn smiled quietly and e–mailed the five scripts to my laptop.

'Got them,' I said. I wanted to finish my tea and read them in bed, something I was used to. I could concentrate there, though it would be different being in Vaughn's bed. I'll just correct that — one of Vaughn's spare bedrooms. He'd suggested I sleep in the room I'd used before to try on the dresses. I was happy to sleep there. It was cosy and luxurious.

While I drank my tea, I read the list of scripts. Two of them were action scripts. A note to Vaughn highlighted they'd like me to work on these. My fighting prowess at the party had been part of the reason these were suggested.

'Why is an advantage for me to be able to fight?'

'As a scriptwriter who is also able to write the action scenes, the fight scenes, as I think you could with your ability in martial arts, this would put you in quite a unique position with this particular production company. Usually they have to hire someone else to write the fight scenes, that's before the script even goes to the movie's fight coordinator. The basic fights are part of the characters and storyline. So if you can do it all, well, you'll earn more money and the script is often better for it.'

'I could rewrite one of these. The espionage one is workable, but the other is tosh. These types of movies never do well.'

'You can't tell him that.'

'Why not?'

'Because they've already optioned the script.'

'They'll lose out financially on this one.'

'It's not your job to tell them that. You have to keep within the perimeters of your brief. They don't like ructions. You won't fit in. It's your job to rewrite the script they've chosen, fix anything that's wrong with it, polish it until it sparkles, and leave the rest to them.'

I nodded.

'I don't mean to sound harsh, Phred, but if you walk into this meeting, you need to be prepared or they'll chew you up.'

'Sounds lovely.'

'You think the newspaper industry is fierce, but the movie world is ferocious.'

I closed my laptop. 'Well, if I'm going to

be back in the circus ring, I'd better get to bed.'

He frowned. 'The circus?'

'Never mind.' Royce had cracked the whip relentlessly at the paper. But by the sounds of it, the snowman was the new ringmaster. I'd be careful what cages I rattled.

'Listen. You can do this. I know you can. I see the potential in you.'

'Why are you so determined to help me, Vaughn? Not that I don't appreciate it.'

He gazed at me, at first with softness in those grey eyes, and then with building passion.

'Because I care about you.'

And then he took be totally unawares.

'Apart from your writing, what do you think about the future? Ever think of settling down?'

'I don't know if I'm the settling down type. But if I met the right man . . .'

'You could be tempted?'

'If he was kind, loyal and honest.'

'I'm tempted to kiss you. Is that honest enough?'

I caught my breath, and nodded.

Vaughn wrapped his arms around me, pulled me close and kissed me. I didn't resist.

His kisses were warm, sensuous, lingering.

Then, still holding me close, he said, 'Tomorrow's meeting is too important. We both need a clear head.'

My head was anything but clear. I could still feel his kiss and the effect he had on me.

'If the meeting goes well, we'll celebrate tomorrow night,' he said, hinting at a romantic evening.

'And I'll kiss you breathless,' I said, smiling.

'Promises, promises . . .' he said, leaving the bedroom.

'Never broken one yet.'

'Goodnight, Phred.'

I went to bed. The blizzard was blowing outside. From the window I could see the snowman we'd built earlier.

I sat up in bed with my laptop. The bed

was luxurious; the duvet and satin quilt were clean and new.

I began reading the scripts. I made a copy of each one and edited them as I went along. Old habits and all that. But if I did get a contract to rewrite these, I'd be ahead of the work. That would surprise them and take the pressure off me. If the meeting bombed and I was never to darken their doors again, then fine, I'd done this work for nothing. I knew with everything that had happened today, leaving the paper, the fight, the meeting tomorrow, and kissing Vaughn, especially kissing him, I'd never sleep tonight, so I'd be as well working. Vaughn's bedroom was downstairs. Mine was on the first floor, so he wouldn't hear me tip tapping away at the keyboard.

I had a habit of ticking over on a couple of hours sleep when things felt pressured. A habit I intended to break. Tonight my bad habit was advantageous. I could tear through two of these scripts by morning. I could.

'Sleep well?' Vaughn said next morning when I went down to the kitchen for breakfast. I'd showered in the en suite bathroom, washed my hair, and tidied myself up. I didn't look tired. The excitement was buzzing through me.

'I was very cosy and comfortable,' I said, not lying, just not giving him the full picture.

'I don't have anything fancy for breakfast,' he said. 'I've made toast and there's cereal. Hope that's okay.'

I pulled up a chair at the breakfast bar, poured myself a glass of fresh orange juice, and had cereal with milk, topped with fruit.

'This is delicious,' I said.

His hair was still damp from showering, and he wore an expensive white shirt and smart black trousers. His tastes were classy but they suited him.

We kind of matched, because I was wearing a white shirt under a black jumper and skinny black trousers tucked into black boots. The white cuffs of the shirt were long and open, adding a bit of style to my outfit.

'You look lovely,' he said. 'Wear that to the meeting. It's ideal. You look like a writer.'

'I do?'

'Yep.'

The kitchen had patio doors that led on to the back garden. I gazed at the beautiful wintry scenes through the glass while I ate my cereal.

'So,' Vaughn said, sounding like he was leading up to something, 'how many scripts did you rewrite while I was sleeping?'

He knew! How did he know?

'Is there any point in lying?'

He shook his head.

I drank some of my tea. 'Two.'

'Only two?'

'And a bit.'

'Hmm. I'm impressed.'

'How did you know?'

'I figured out the formula while I was lying in bed. Phred plus bed plus laptop plus scripts needing rewritten equals — a hell of a lot of writing done in the night.'

I had another sip of tea. Vaughn drank coffee.

Then we both laughed.

'I don't ever want you to work at that rate,' he said, 'but I'll be honest with you. Just this once, if you can hand those over today at the meeting, I'd say the contract will be yours.'

'One of the scripts only needed four scenes rewritten. That was a couple of hours work.'

'Well, I think they'll be impressed.'

After breakfast, I made more tea and coffee and we went through to the lounge. We chatted about the scripts, and then Vaughn had work to do and left me to write in the lounge while he worked in his office.

There was no mention of our kissing but I could sense the attraction between us. But more than anything, it felt heart warming to be treated with some kindness. I'd become so used to the sarcasm and snide remarks from Royce the ringmaster, that backbiting and harshness had become the norm. That was wrong on so many levels. This morning was like taking the blinkers off and realising how things could be. Yes, I was sitting in a millionaire's mansion, not worrying about the heating bills and rent for the first time in . . . maybe ever, but it felt more normal with simple things like having tea and cereal for breakfast.

Bradley's world with his glitzy parties was anything but normal, and yet I was comfortable with him. I'd never cared what anyone said, rich or poor, if you find someone you're comfortable with, that friend is worth their weight in gold.

But I'd no intention of dropping my guard yet. If I treated this meeting as if it was a fiery day at the newspaper office, hopefully I'd come out unscathed.

Vaughn cleared the snow from his car and we got ready to drive to the meeting. The car had been sitting in the snow since last night. When he tried to fire up the engine, the car wouldn't start.

Concerned we'd be late for the meeting, I got out of the car. He wondered what I was doing, and it crossed my mind that we should use my car, but I decided to see if I could get his started.

'Pop the bonnet open,' I called to him through the window. It had stopped snowing but it was freezing cold.

Vaughn clicked it open. 'What are you doing?'

'Tinkering with it,' I said. 'Okay, try it now.'

He did, and the car started up.

I closed the bonnet and got back into the car, shivering slightly.

Vaughn was laughing at what I'd just done as he revved up the engine and we were on our way.

We arrived for the meeting with the producer at his Manhattan office. There were two sides to the company — movie production and property.

The producer (I kept thinking of him as the snowman), a director, a production assistant and Vaughn and me sat around a large table. The office had an expansive view of New York. I could see the newspaper building a few blocks away. I wondered what they would be doing. What I would be doing if I was still there? Was it really only yesterday that I'd walked away from the paper?

The first thing we discussed was Bradley's script, the one I'd doctored. They confirmed what they'd said in the e–mail, that it had been approved, and they were paying me, as Bradley had promised, and crediting me as one of the scriptwriters.

So now I had the ten thousand dollars, plus the additional payment, and I had the money from the paparazzi work.

I planned to buy one treat, a few necessities and save the rest in case everything went to rats. The treat would be a camera. Strangely, I missed the paparazzi camera. And I wanted a new duvet and covers for my bed. A nice big fluffy duvet and pillows so that I could sit up in bed with my laptop and write the scripts.

The producer was talking. 'We'd like you to work on a few scripts. One of them, the espionage screenplay, we want it in a hurry. If you can finish it in three days we'll pay you fifteen thousand dollars. If you finish it in two days, we'll pay double.'

'What if I gave you the script now?' I said.

The producer blinked. 'I'd write you a blank cheque.'

'Make it payable to Phred. I'm waiving my fee on this,' said Vaughn.

The producer leaned forward. 'You've finished it?'

'I worked on it last night. I changed a few of the main scenes. The rest seemed okay.'

Vaughn e–mailed the script to the producer's assistant whose laptop was on the table.

‘And I’ll e–mail the other one that she’s finished,’ said Vaughn.

‘She’s finished another one?’ the director said, looking in surprise at the producer.

I nodded.

‘If we approve these,’ said the producer. ‘You’ll be well paid. In the meantime, can you start work on the other three projects?’

I hesitated.

‘Something up?’ the producer said.

‘I’m interested in two of the scripts, but the third one . . . ’ I glanced at Vaughn whose eyes were willing me not to tell the truth. The producer sensed the tension.

‘Speak up, Phred. Say what you think,’ the producer said.

‘It won’t work. Movies with those types of themes and storylines are never successful, and yet people keep making them. Name me any in the past few years that have been box office hits.’

The producer looked at the director.

‘Could you rewrite it?’ the director said to

me.

'It still wouldn't work. What matters is when people are in the cinema, bums on seats, whether they enjoy it. People don't like these movies.'

The producer nodded. 'She's right. I've been thinking this myself. She's the only one to say what needed said.' He said to me, 'You've just saved us at least $30 million in pre production costs.' He looked at Vaughn. 'We'll have to figure out some form of payment for that.'

'Does it have to be in money?' I said.

'What other form of payment did you have in mind?' the producer said.

I liked him. He was sharp. He didn't play games.

'I'm looking for somewhere to live. A house, with a garden. In New York. You have property. Houses to lease.'

'You want a house?'

'The lease of it for free.'

'For how long?'

‘One year.’

‘Done.’

‘Thank you,’ I said.

He nodded that he was happy with the deal. He stood up. The meeting was almost over.

‘Remind me to let you make the deals from now on,’ Vaughn whispered to me.

‘Sorry, I know you could’ve handled it, but I’m used to dealing with things on my own.’

‘Don’t ever lose that ability,’ said Vaughn.

The producer buttoned the jacket of his suit. ‘I’ll have the contracts drawn up and get them to you by the end of the day.’

‘Great,’ said Vaughn.

We all shook hands.

‘Welcome to our world,’ the producer said to me.

As he said this, I saw the newspaper building in the distance. Despite everything, I felt my heart ache that it was gone.

I saw Vaughn put together my thoughts. 'You made the right decision, Phred.'

I nodded. I had made the right decision. I just wished I didn't feel so sad about it.

Vaughn and I went to my apartment to pick up some of my own scripts that I didn't have on my laptop. He wanted to read them after we'd had dinner at his house.

Vaughn looked around. 'I'd hoped to say that this apartment was okay. Homely maybe, but it's not. You can't stay here, Phred.'

'I'll stay until I get the house.'

'You could stay with me.'

'I'd never get any work done. I'm going to start on the scripts tonight. Besides, I can afford to heat this place, and I'm used to it. I'll write quicker here.'

'Okay. But you're still having dinner at my house.'

I picked up the scripts.

'I'll even bake a cake,' I said.

The snowman was waiting for us. The frosty one, not the producer. I shook the fresh snow off his scarf and tidied him up as I went by. He was frozen solid.

While Vaughn dealt with catching up on some business calls for his clients, I made dinner and baked a cake. A Victoria sponge with buttercream filling, raspberry jam, and white icing.

'Smells delicious in here,' Vaughn said, coming into the kitchen carrying his laptop.

'Dinner's almost ready.'

Vaughn smiled at me. 'You've been offered the choice of ten properties.' He handed the laptop to me.

I put the laptop down on the kitchen counter, and my jaw dropped when I saw what was listed. Photographs of each house showed beautiful mansion style homes that looked like they were out of some exclusive estate agents listing. And I supposed they were.

I couldn't take my eyes of them. 'I can have any one of these?'

'You can view them tomorrow.'

We had dinner, and then Vaughn drove me round that night to see the houses. He seemed as excited as I was, and I couldn't wait to see them. 'All of them are great, but this is it. It's got the right feel to it. I love it. It's perfect.'

The house was smaller than Vaughn and Bradley's houses, but a mansion in normal terms. The garden had trees around the front and back lawns that were covered in snow. The property was a lovely mix of traditional and modern, with large windows that would let lots of light in.

'We'll view it inside in the morning,' he said.

I nodded, jumped up and threw my arms around him. He swung me round and round in the snow in front of the house that was to become my home for the next year.

We went back to Vaughn's house for cake, though I'd made him drive past the new property three times before we headed back.

I snuggled on the sofa near the fire and

viewed photographs of the house on my laptop. It was in the same upmarket area as Vaughn's. The description said that the house was semi–furnished which was exactly what I wanted. If I had the basics, I could make it what I needed. It had four bedrooms, so that gave me three spare rooms to use as an office or writing room, a room to set up as an art studio (always wanted one of those), and a dressmaking room. I hadn't done any sewing since I arrived in New York and it was something I used to enjoy. I planned to pick up a sewing machine, and the thought of it filled me with excitement. And I had a brilliant excuse — with all the parties Bradley had I'd need plenty of dresses. If I made my own it would save me from dressing up as an alien.

In my mind, all the rooms were accounted for, including the lounge which was a long room from the front window to the patio doors leading on to the garden. The polished wood floor would be ideal for dancing, and I could practise my martial arts.

No furniture was in it and I was intended keeping it like that. It would be like a dance studio. A smaller lounge was on the ground floor and it seemed cosier, so I'd use it for relaxing and for writing.

The kitchen was wonderful, and my bedroom, which was furnished in creams and pale lemon, had an en suite bathroom. The rooms were carpeted or had wood floors, and the colour scheme was creams and neutrals.

I closed the laptop when Vaughn brought tea, coffee and cake through. We relaxed by the fire and I felt myself unwinding.

Then Vaughn came over and sat beside me. 'You were impressive today at the meeting. Later, I'd like to read your scripts, your original work. But first, I was wondering if I could take you up on that promise of yours?'

I leaned close. 'What promise would that be?'

His reply was to kiss me.

Vaughn's kisses were warm and sensual. I could've kissed him for hours, and probably would have, but as I snuggled beside him on the big, comfy sofa watching the fire flicker, he fell asleep. I fell asleep too, and we both woke up early the next morning. We hadn't gotten up to anything except kissing, but I felt more relaxed than I had in a long time.

Vaughn had a busy day of meetings with clients ahead of him. He jumped in the shower, ate a hasty breakfast, and apologised that he couldn't view the house with me until the afternoon. I told him this was fine.

After he left, I phoned the contact for the house leasing. They turned up within the hour. The house was as perfect as I'd hoped, and I told them I'd take it there and then. They sent round hospitality packs and other stuff. Two huge hampers of food, new bed linen, and other things that sorted out the basics. By lunchtime I'd moved in.

By three in the afternoon, I'd packed my belongings from my old apartment, said goodbye to it, and drove to my new house. I didn't own a lot, in fact, everyone I had in the world fitted easily into my car with room to spare.

I was dancing in the lounge, trying out the long wooden floor, when Bradley arrived. I heard him tip– tapping on the window. He waved at me, and I ran excitedly to let him in.

He'd brought cake, and champagne and glasses.

I had a glass of champagne to celebrate.

'If there's anything you need to help you get settled in, let me know,' he said.

I gave him a huge hug.

And then he joined me on the dance floor, swirling me round and round.

We were still laughing when Vaughn arrived. He loved that I'd moved into the house and that I seemed happy. But then he frowned.

'I have to catch a flight out to Hollywood tonight,' Vaughn said to me. 'I'll be gone two or three days at the most.'

'That's fine,' I said. After all, he was a Hollywood agent, who split his time between New York and Los Angeles.

'Call me if you need me. I don't want you to think you're left alone to get on with things.' He sounded concerned, and cursed the bad timing of having to make the trip to Los Angeles.

'I'll make sure she misbehaves while you're away,' said Bradley.

Vaughn smiled. 'I don't doubt it.'

We said goodbye at the front door. 'You know how I feel about you, Phred.'

I did.

'I don't like leaving you here alone,' he murmured, pulling me close to him.

'There nothing wrong with being alone, Vaughn. There's only something wrong when you can't cope with it, but that's never been my problem.'

He nodded.

'Besides, you'd just be a distraction, and I want to get these scripts written.' I smiled at him.

'I've packed your two scripts in my bag. I'll read them when I'm in LA.' He kissed me, and then he was gone, driving off into the night.

Chapter Eight

On The Wrong Side Of The Camera Again

I was up bright and early and drove into the centre of New York. Manhattan was still iced with snow, and I'd wrapped up warm with a white hat, scarf and gloves, and a black wool jacket I'd found in my wardrobe during the move.

I'd worked like a demon on the scripts the previous night, and was well ahead of my deadline schedules. So . . . this morning I was going shopping.

A camera was first on my list. The treat I'd promised myself. I went to a shop near the newspaper office. It sold all sorts of cameras. I chose the same model I'd used when working as the paparazzi. I'd liked it, so I splashed out and treated myself to one of those.

I left the shop, admiring my new

purchase, when a ghost of the past walked right up to me.

'Hello, Phred.'

I looked up, and reeled back when I saw who it was. 'Finbar.' My stomach jolted, and I didn't know whether to smile or run.

'I heard you got the flick from the newspaper.'

'Charming as ever.'

'I was there this morning. I wondered why your features weren't in the paper. I thought maybe there was something up.'

I blinked. This information did not compute.

'Not that I've been spying on you, but it's hard not to be tempted to read your stuff in the press.'

'You're living in New York?' I said, still trying to get my thoughts around the fact that he was standing there. He'd hardly changed. If anything, he looked more affluent than ever, and as a pub owner he'd done very well for himself. The black hair was sexy wild and long enough to touch the collar of his dark coat. The green eyes had lost none of their roguish twinkle, and he spoke in a rich, Dublin accent, frequently smiling and in perpetual motion, moving from one foot to the other, the boxer in him never still.

'Yes, I'm opening a pub in New York with another couple of investors from Dublin. Expanding our interests across the pond. The pubs back home have done well, so I'm putting some of the profits into opening one here. I've got the premises. It'll be open in a few days.'

'How long have you been in city?'

'A couple of months. I kept meaning to chap your door, but I've been busy, and I wanted to wait until the pub was ready. And surprise you by inviting you to the grand opening.'

He stopped talking long enough to take a breath and glance up at the newspaper building.

'Royce is a fucking arsehole by the way.'

'You spoke to Royce?'

'I've just been into the newspaper office asking about you. I told him I was the ex love of your life, and demanded to know what was what. He said you'd more or less told him to stuff his paparazzi work up his arse and light it. Smarmy bastard. I was tempted to punch his fuckin' lights out.'

He looked at the camera around my neck. 'So are you working as the paparazzi for another paper now?'

'No.'

'Then what's with the camera?'

'I bought it this morning to make me feel better.'

'Are you strapped for cash?' he said, taking his wallet from his coat pocket. His wallet was thick with cash.

'I'm okay for money,' I said.

'You know I'd give you my last penny. Of course, then I'd have to borrow it back to open up a pub.'

He'd never been tight fisted with money. In fact, he was extremely generous.

'Look, I made a big mistake with you in Dublin. But I'm a changed man. I'm thirty–three years old.'

'Thirty–two.'

'Am I? Jeezo, you're right. Well, anyway. I'd like to find myself a wife and get married.'

I laughed. 'I can't see you ever settling down.'

'I want to get married but I don't want to settle down. When two people who love each other get married, there should be double the fun. If you and I got married, we'd be out enjoying ourselves, driving across America, flying back and forth to Dublin, swimming in the sea in the rain, and dancing through the night.'

'Well, with a wallet full of money like that, I'm sure you'll find yourself a wife in New York.'

'I don't want someone who is just after my money. Or a walking wardrobe that looks great but has nothing to say for herself.'

'I really have to go,' I said, making a

move to walk away.

'Give me your phone number so we can keep in touch.'

'I don't think that's a good idea.'

'I won't pester you. I've been in New York for two months and I haven't caused you any trouble now have I?'

I shrugged. This was true.

'Give me your number. I'll find you anyway. You know I will.'

Finbar had a knack for finding anyone anywhere. 'You should've opened a detective agency rather than a pub.' I gave him my number and he gave me his.

'You're looking gorgeous by the way. I like your hat. You used to have some lovely hats.' He smiled so bright and without any hint of guile. 'It's great to see you again. It really is.'

My mouth wouldn't form the words to return the compliment.

He moved closer, smiling as if the sun was shining.

'Give me a kiss.'

‘Get away’.

‘Come on, you know I’m the best kisser you ever had.’

‘Not any more.’

‘Oh. Who is the lucky man that’s stolen my thunder?’

I didn’t answer.

‘Ah, you’re fibbing. There’s no one,’ he said. ‘If I know you Phred, you’ll have been working your arse off and nothing else. I can see I’m right.’

I still didn’t answer.

‘Come on, give me a kiss. I’ll make you forget all the bad.’

‘No, and I mean no.’

He grabbed me and forced a kiss on my lips.

I pushed him back. He was laughing and moving in to kiss me again. So I gave him a back hand strike across his face. Instead of the usual slap to the face with the palm, I used the back of my hand — like a back hander only with technique. I hit him clean, the sound of the strike like a crack in the cold air. It didn't do any real damage, nor was it intended to. But the side of his face began to swell like a balloon, his eye started to close, though I could still see the steely glint in it.

The only way to deal with this was to apply a cold compress, or ice, or . . .

So there was Finbar lying with his face in the snow drift.

'You always were a fucking challenge, Phred.'

'Good luck opening your new bar.'

'I know you still like me.'

'You know nothing.'

I got in my car and drove off.

Determined not to let Finbar's return spoil things, I continued my shopping spree. Spree is perhaps too grand a word, conjuring up images of being laden down with a dozen bags filled with clothes, shoes and other frippery. Spree in my sense was a couple of hats and new fleecy socks for dancing in my lounge.

A favourite little vintage shop of mine, tucked into a niche in the city, was next on my list. They had hats, and I tried on numerous styles, colours and fabrics. I bought two woolly hats including a lovely cream one, and a colourful one with pom poms. And some fleecy socks. I also had a look through the racks of vintage evening and cocktail dresses, wondering if I should buy one. Bradley was sure to have another party, and I didn't want to be the one frock wonder. I chose a sparkly cocktail dress that had a drop waist, giving it a flapper style vibe. Very reasonably priced. I tried it on and realised I'd have to alter it slightly to fit, but that was something else on my list — a sewing kit. I bought a sewing kit in a fabric shop, along with a few metres of material (including white jersey silk, deep blue chiffon and bronze velvet), and a basic sewing machine. So I guess that would qualify as a spree after all.

I put everything in the boot of my car, had tea and toffee cake in a cafe, and then went ice skating in the park. Having shopped, skated and slapped Finbar in the face, I drove home to work on the scripts.

I worked for six hours solid on the scripts and finished them. I planned to work on my own screenplays next. The two scripts Vaughn had taken with him to Hollywood were screenplays I'd written previously, and I wanted to write new scripts. I had a few ideas, and typed rough notes into my laptop while dinner was cooking.

I ate dinner in the kitchen and thought about Vaughn. He'd be in Hollywood by now. I wondered if I should tell him that Finbar had kissed me. He'd only been gone a day and already my ex had tried to snog me in the middle of Manhattan.

I pulled the laptop nearer and searched the web for information about Finbar. And sure enough, he had a website advertising his Dublin pubs, and news of his new pub in New York. So he had been telling the truth.

I was building a snowman in the front garden

that night when a car pulled up outside my house. The headlights flicked off, and I saw that it was Royce. I scooped a large handful of snow and armed myself with a snowball.

He got out of the car and walked over to me. His coat was buttoned up and he wore a warm scarf. I'd never seen him wear a scarf before. Perhaps my woolly hat was breeding overnight in his desk drawer and producing knitwear.

'You're building a snowman,' he said, as if by saying it he'd comprehend that it was true.

I cupped the snowball, rolling it from one hand to the other, pressing it into a hard ball of solid snow.

'Your crazy ex–boyfriend was in the office today. One of the subs was going to throw him out.'

'I wouldn't advise that. Finbar is a former boxer. He was tempted to punch your lights out.'

Royce nodded thoughtfully.

'You drove all the way here to tell me about Finbar?' I said. 'You could've phoned or e–mailed.'

'I brought you something.' He pulled my woolly hat, the one he'd confiscated, from his coat pocket and handed it to me.

He glanced at the new colourful woolly hat I'd bought earlier. I'd worn it to keep warm while building the snowman. He made no comment, but I could see him looking at my pom poms.

'One of the guys, a reporter, wrote the motoring feature. He took the car for a test drive, thrashed the life out of it, and the car company aren't happy with the feature he wrote. And they say he's ruined the car's suspension. So basically the feature was shit. I'm not offering you your old job back, but I wondered if you'd still like to do the car features. The motoring supplement for the paper is due in December. I'd like you to write it.'

'No, that's not for me.'

He nodded again.

'Have dinner with me sometime when you don't hate me so bad,' he said.

'That could take a while.'

'I can wait. Though remember I retire in twenty years time.' He breathed in the cold night air. 'I have to get back to the office. I wanted to give you your hat, tell you about your crazy ex boyfriend, and . . .'

He walked away to his car, and then said over his shoulder, 'Have you read the paper today?'

I had bought a copy, but it lay in the kitchen unread. I was in the habit of reading it in the morning in the office during our 'oh shit' meetings. When the paper came out and it was too late to change anything, the subs, reporters, and Royce would open the newspaper on their desks and scan it for any errors or gaffs. Cries of, 'Oh shit,' would be heard, as they read their mistakes, missing pieces or wrong captions and headlines. Certainly, there were numerous times when the paper came out perfect. But the 'Oh shit' meetings were legendary.

'No, I haven't read today's paper,' I said.

Royce got into his car and said through the open window. 'You should —you're in it.' He drove off before I could ask him what I'd done.

I hurried into the house and flicked through the paper. One of the headlines said, 'Paparazzo punches Irish tourist.' The editorial, which was slight, accompanied a photograph of Finbar smiling at the camera, his face half swollen. There was also a blurry pic of me shoving his face in the snow. I was being helpful. I was. Luckily I wasn't named in the paper.

I thought it was ridiculous. Finbar could take a real crack on the jaw and not flinch. Someone had slanted the whole incident. They must have seen us from the windows of the paper or been lurking nearby. Maybe it was someone from the paparazzi?

I sighed wearily.

I was on the wrong side of the camera again.

Chapter Nine

I'd Marry You Tomorrow

'I told the press nothing,' Finbar said, when I phoned and accused him of being a manipulative, publicity hungry weasel.

'You told them about your new pub opening.'

'They asked me what I was doing in Manhattan.'

'And you posed for the photograph, showing off your swollen face and smiling for them.'

'I did not. When you flounced off to your car, I lay there in the snow, and the paparazzi came at me and flashed their cameras. I couldn't stop them.'

'Why were you smiling?'

'I wasn't smiling. They accidentally kicked me in the balls. I was grimacing.'

I studied the photograph. Hmm, it

could've been a grimace.

'I'd never risk a publicity stunt just when you and me are about to get back together.'

'Hold on there. We're not getting back together.'

'I can hear you're distraught, so we'll talk later.'

'No, I'm not interested in getting back together with you.'

'Okay. But come down to the bar tonight. I'll give you the grand tour.'

I hesitated.

'I could do with your help with the cocktail menu. Remember the last one you made? I still use that in the bars in Dublin.'

'I made some of them up.'

'That's why there's nothing like them anywhere else.'

I was still reluctant to drive down to his bar.

'At least have a look over the press release. It could make or break the launch. You always wrote brilliant press releases.'

‘Why should I help you, Finbar?’

‘Because you’re a better person than I am. Please, Phred, give me a hand with the press release.’

‘Tell me the address,’ I said.

‘How did you end up as a paparazzo?’ Finbar said as we sat together at the bar. The premises seemed almost ready for customers. The bar was well stocked and lit with spotlights.

‘Royce needed me to cover Bradley Goldsilver’s movie premier. I got inveigled. And all of a sudden — oops! I’m the paparazzi.’

He gave me a wicked grin. ‘I saw your poms poms in the newspaper and on the television. I was cheering you on. Go Phred!’

We smiled at each other.

‘Anyway, I only did a few paparazzi assignments, but it caused me nothing but trouble. Then Royce wanted me to do them full time and . . .’

‘You told him to stick them and light them.’

‘Sort of. But the paparazzi work is how I met Bradley,’ I said. ‘If Royce hadn’t sent me to the premier, I’d still be jumping through hoops of fire every day at the newspaper with Royce the ringmaster cracking the whip.’

‘So you’re friends with the film star and his Hollywood agent?’

‘Yes. I’m doing scriptwriting now. Doctoring up scripts they need improved and rewritten. The money is terrific, and I’ve got a lovely house rent free for a year as part of the deal.’

‘Which one is the great kisser?’

‘Vaughn, the agent.’

His tone deepened. ‘Do you think if I gave you time, I could make things right between us again?’

I chose my words carefully. Finbar was really trying to be sweet, and despite everything, it was so nice to see a face from home after all this time.

‘I’m happy with Vaughn,’ I said.

Finbar looked disheartened, and then he

forced himself to brighten up. 'Will you run your eye over the press release?'

'Yes.'

I sat at the bar and rewrote it on my laptop while he took a phone call in his office.

'Jeezo, that was fast,' he said when he came back. 'You need to slow down. You'll end up meeting yourself coming out the door when you're on your way in.'

'I know.'

He put the drinks menu notes down on the bar. 'I'll make us a pot of tea. If you can have the cocktail menu done by the time the kettle boils I'd appreciate it.'

I laughed.

'I'm glad we're talking again,' he said, and went off to make the tea.

I started putting ideas down for the cocktails. Things like this were always fun to write.

Finbar came back with the tea and chocolate cake, and set it down on the bar. 'Happy birthday, Phred.'

My snowman was glistening in the dark when I got home.

I parked my car, went inside, picked up my camera, and went back out to photograph the snowman, and the house, which looked picturesque in the snow. I didn't know how long all this would last, and I wanted to make sure I had photographs of it. As I photographed the house from all angles, I hadn't realised how bright the flash was in the dark. It lit up the building, and alerted the neighbours who peered from their windows wondering what was going on.

I flicked the camera off and hurried inside. By morning the gossip would've circulated that the paparazzi had moved in.

An e–mail from Vaughn asked how I was getting on, and whether I was behaving myself. I replied, assuring him I was up to mischief.

I think he assumed I was joking, but at least I hadn't lied.

He told me he missed me, and was looking forward to coming home.

I padded through to the kitchen in my new fluffy socks and flicked the kettle on to make a tea before going to bed.

Then I snuggled up in bed, with my laptop, and began fleshing out the script notes I'd written earlier. I wrote twenty pages of my new script before falling asleep. I had a dream about the story, and I rattled it into the laptop when I woke up before the thoughts faded. This meant I'd even managed to work in my sleep.

By lunch time I'd written the first fifty pages of my script, basing the lead character on Bradley. I'd a clear image of Bradley in my mind, and this helped me with characterisation. I doubted this was something that would ever go into production, or star Bradley, but I felt the urge to get it down while it was fresh and exciting.

I also had a final read over the scripts I'd rewritten for the producer, and then e–mailed them off to him. He acknowledged he'd received them, and from what he'd read they were ideal. So everything was hunky–dory with that.

Later, Bradley called, inviting me to a party at his house at eight. I said I'd be there, and then I set about making a dress. It was almost seven–thirty. Although I had the sewing machine, there was no time to use it for dressmaking. All I needed was the white jersey silk material — and a stapler.

I'd used this method before – twice – and it had worked just fine. The dress wouldn't stand up to scrutiny, but I was sure it would be perfect for tonight.

I wrapped the material (which was the size of a large bath towel) around myself, tied two ends in a knot, making the start of a halter neck and low backed dress. Judging how far I wanted the cleavage to show (not much), I stapled the front of the dress together, leaving a split at the hem. Then came the finicky part, reaching round to the lower back, making tucks and stapling them so that the back started to fit the waist. Once that was done, I tied a soft, wide silver belt around the waist to hide the staples, stepped into a pair of evening shoes, pinned my hair up with a large silver clasp, applied mascara and lip gloss, picked up my clutch bag and off I went to Bradley's party.

'You look great,' Bradley said, greeting me with a hug.

'Just beware of the staples,' I said, giving him a sneak peek under my belt.

'You stapled a dress together?' He started to laugh.

'Ssh! Keep your voice down. You didn't exactly give me much warning that you were having a party, and I didn't have time to sew one or alter the dress I bought today.'

'This is the last big promo party, so things should start to quieten down.'

'Cutting back to three parties a week instead of six?'

We were laughing when the producer

(snowman) approached us. 'I've finished reading the scripts you rewrote and they're wonderful,' he said to me. He looked around. 'Where's Vaughn?'

I frowned. 'He's in Hollywood. I thought you knew.'

The producer shook his head. 'No, but never mind, I'll talk to him when he gets back.' And off he went.

'Don't be suspicious,' said Bradley. 'I'm sure Vaughn can explain.'

I nodded. Maybe he had another reason for being in Hollywood.

During the party, a man tried to chat me up. Bradley had a word with him.

'What did you say to him?'

'I said that you are involved with Vaughn. You are together?'

'I'd like to think so.'

Bradley smiled. 'Find another one of you for me, Phred.'

'One magnet for trouble is enough, don't you think?' I said.

'At least you're not boring. I read about you in the paper today,' he said. 'Congratulations.'

'It's not something I want to celebrate.'

'I thought you'd be pleased to win.'

'Win?'

'Winning the paparazzi photograph of the year in your newspaper.'

My heart jolted. 'Do you have a copy of the paper?'

He did. We went to his office to read it.

I flicked through the paper, and there it was. Ten photographs were nominated. Readers of the paper had voted online yesterday for their favourite, and the winner was in today's paper. The picture I'd taken in the nightclub, the one with Bradley and the celebrities jumping up into the air, was the winner. There was no prize, just the honour and prestige of winning.

'It's a wonderful photo,' said Bradley.

I nodded. Despite leaving the paper, I was still associated with the paparazzi.

I flicked through the paper again and found the picture of Finbar. 'This is my ex–boyfriend, Finbar, the one I told you about from Dublin.'

'What happened to his face?' Bradley said. 'Why is he grimacing?'

'I slapped his face.'

Bradley tried not to laugh. 'He looks like a troublemaker. I'm sure he deserved it. But what did he do?'

'He kissed me.'

'Does Vaughn know?'

I shook my head, and explained everything that had happened with Finbar.

'So now you've created his cocktail menus?' Bradley said. 'And you're friends again.'

'Just friends.'

'When does this bar of his open in New York?'

'In a couple of days. I wrote his press release, and he's e–mailing that out to the papers. Frankly, I don't know if they'll give him any publicity. Another bar opening in the city isn't that newsworthy.'

'Hmm?'

'What?' I said.

'I'd be happy to go to the launch night and bring a few friends if that would help you.'

'You'd do that?'

'It might be fun. In the meantime, I'd like to try one of those cocktails you mentioned.' And off we went, through to the bar.

Bradley wouldn't stop singing. I blame the fourth cocktail he insisted on having. He was still singing as I left the party and headed home.

Vaughn had e–mailed. He would be home in two days. The same day as Finbar's launch party. I wondered how he'd feel about going with me. Although I wasn't planning to frequent the bar, I'd promised to go to the launch. But Vaughn might not want to meet my ex–boyfriend.

I worked on my new script the next day, and by the time Vaughn was due back, I'd finished the first draft. Putting it aside, I got ready to welcome Vaughn home.

His car pulled up in the driveway. He smiled when he saw me.

He had a present for me, wrapped in gold paper with a gold bow.

'What is it?' I said.

'It's part of the real reason I made the trip to LA,' he said. 'I didn't want to tell you and get your hopes up in case the deal didn't happen.'

'What deal?'

'Open it,' he said, handing me the present.

I peeled the paper off to find one of my scripts he'd taken with him to Hollywood. I didn't understand.

'Look inside the script,' he said.

I opened it, and found a contract inside. Skimming what it said, it began to dawn on me that Vaughn had sold my script to a film studio in Hollywood.

'Is this what I think it is?' I said.

'Yes, I've sold one of your scripts.'

I jumped up and threw my arms around him.

'Your spy drama is outstanding,' he said. 'I knew I could sell it. It'll make a great movie.'

We talked for an hour or so about his trip, the meetings, and people he'd spoken to. And of course about selling my script. He'd just given a lot more financial security, and the chance to write my own scripts rather than rewrite other people's scripts. Not that I was complaining at all about the latter.

'So what have you been up to?' he said.

'I've been busy.'

By the time I got to the part about slapping Finbar, the story being in the newspaper, winning the paparazzi photograph award, creating the cocktail list, writing the press release, e–mailing the scripts to the producer, building a snowman, buying hats, and a camera, skating in the park, wearing a stapled dress to Bradley's party, getting him drunk on cocktails, and writing a new script, it was time to get ready for Finbar's launch party.

'Do you want to come to the launch party? Bradley will be there with some of his friends.'

'I wouldn't miss it,' said Vaughn.

Unless I was mistaken, there was a steely glint in Vaughn's eyes. Maybe it was jet lag. Maybe it was jealousy. I had a hunch I'd find out when he met Finbar.

The launch party was quite busy. The bar was lively with people enjoying themselves. We arrived at the same time as Bradley and several of his friends. Most of them were actors and directors. Unfortunately, the press weren't interested in the bar launch and no journalists or photographers had turned up. I thought this was a total waste of good celebrities, so I got my camera from Vaughn's car (I'd brought it just in case) and became the paparazzi.

Customers were delighted to mingle with the well known actors. Bradley was particularly friendly and signed lots of autographs and chatted to fans. I snapped numerous pictures and planned to send them to the newspapers myself. I even took some exclusive pictures for Royce's paper. I hoped this would encourage him to publish them.

I introduced Finbar to Bradley and Vaughn.

'You're the movie star,' Finbar said to Bradley, 'so you must be the agent,' he said to Vaughn.

Then Finbar and Vaughn did one of those handshakes where they lock palms and squeeze until they almost break each others fingers.

I don't know how the antagonism between Vaughn and Finbar escalated so quickly, but soon they were involved in an arm wrestling match and lots of others wanted to join in.

Back in Dublin, Finbar was always arm

wrestling, fighting and fooling around. His years of boxing training had given him sinewy muscles like steel, and he'd been known to beat men who were a lot heavier. He took his jacket off and rolled up the sleeves of his black shirt until the fabric was tight on his upper arms, making his biceps bulge in readiness. He shook his body, loosening up as if it was a championship fight, so this was not going to end well. Finbar rarely took anything seriously, but when he did you could stand by.

I didn't know what Vaughn's prowess was, but I was surprised when he rolled up his white shirt sleeves to reveal arms that looked like contenders.

Bradley glanced at me, and I got the impression that he was as surprised as I was at Vaughn's eagerness to participate. I thought that this was probably not an encouraging sign. Finbar was used to rough and tumble, but Vaughn seemed to live in a world of Hollywood business. As he'd said himself, he didn't do any fitness training to keep in shape.

Though he was adept at press–ups, which he'd done in the snow the day we built the snowman in the garden. I'd had to take my jacket off and put in quite a bit of effort to beat him. Maybe that's why his throwing arm was weakened for the snowball fight. However, Vaughn was well up for the arm wrestling, even though from the betting that had started, the sure money was on the Irish ex–boxer. But as a prime example of a wild card myself, I'd never underestimate the outsider.

I got the camera ready.

Bradley got roped in as the referee. Soon he got caught up in the excitement, and posed between Finbar and Vaughn so I could take a photograph before the challenge kicked off.

Loads of people crowded round and the bar's security guys had to move them back to give Finbar and Vaughn room to breathe. One of the bar tables and two chairs were set up, with the challengers eyeballing each other across the table. Bradley explained the rules. Basically, keep their elbows on the table, and no dirty tricks.

Finbar and Vaughn clasped hands, straining at the starting point, knuckles tight, the veins in their forearms standing out already, elbows on the table.

Bradley gave the signal to start, and both men applied the pressure, hoping to beat their opponent in a speedy bout. But they were evenly matched, and held each other's efforts off.

The shouts and cheers raged around me, becoming louder when Finbar gained the upper hand and began to push Vaughn's hand down towards the table. I hadn't realised I'd shouted, 'No!' so loud until Vaughn flicked a glance at me, and encouraged by my cry, fought back, pushing Finbar's hand up, over and then down towards the table. I swear I saw the whites of Finbar's eyes as he strained with all his sinew.

The excitement was building. Bradley punched the air with tightly clenched fists, urging them on.

I clicked the camera, taking photographs,

trying to include Bradley in them — looking for the gold dust shot. And then it came . . .

I got a picture of Vaughn almost overpowering Finbar, with Bradley's face in the shot, acting as the referee. A movie star, a Hollywood agent, and a Dublin bar owner in New York. This was the type of picture that newspapers would love.

Finbar fought back, refusing to be beaten, and I was beginning to think that one of them would break their arm rather than lose.

Luckily, a giant plastic shamrock, part of the decor, fell down from the ceiling and hit Finbar like a bowling ball striking a skittle. Poor Finbar. He was knocked for six. But again, luckily, he'd a soft landing on the carpet, and having been knocked down before in the boxing ring, he bounced back up, loosening up, shaking off the blow and eager for a rematch.

This is where I stepped in and declared a draw. Someone had to. Bradley agreed, and as he was the referee, his decision was final.

Everyone cheered. Finbar and Vaughn had indeed been equally strong and tenacious. No shame to either of them. It would be an event that would be talked about for many a year in Finbar's pub. A story for the archives. When the gold dust shot came out in the press, I was sure Finbar would frame the newspaper cutting and it would be hung in pride of place above the bar.

Finbar offered his hand to Vaughn who was happy to shake on it.

'So when are you marrying my girlfriend?' Finbar said to Vaughn.

Uh–oh. The touch paper was lit again.

'I was thinking next summer. I'll send you an invitation so you can buy a hat,' said Vaughn.

'Right,' I said stepping in. 'That's enough silly talk. Play nice.' I pulled Vaughn away.

In a quieter corner I shook my head at Vaughn. 'You'll have to learn not to encourage him. Finbar has no off switch. He'll just keep going until he wins.'

‘He didn’t win tonight,’ said Vaughn.

‘You’re all pumped up with adrenalin and talking shite,’ I told him.

He smiled and pulled me close. ‘I love it when you’re all fiery.’

‘I’ll give you fiery if you pull another stunt like that. I’ve certainly seen another side to you tonight.’

‘Good or bad?’

‘I’ll have to sleep on it,’ I said.

He gave me the sexiest of smiles. ‘That can be arranged.’

I shook my head. ‘Two words — newspaper photographs.’

Vaughn sighed. ‘Can’t blame a man for trying.’

‘Never have, never will.’ I said. ‘Now I have to get these photographs and story to the papers before anyone else tips them off.’

‘That’s right, I forgot you’re the paparazzi,’ he said, teasing me.

‘Award winning paparazzi,’ I said, joining in the joke.

We said goodnight to Bradley and his friends, who were enjoying themselves, but Finbar was surrounded by people lauding him for his arm wrestling, and I couldn't get near him.

Vaughn and I left the bar. The snow was beginning to melt, turning to slush, and a misty rain made the lights from the bars and businesses a blur of colourful reflections.

The car was parked across the street. Vaughn wrapped his arms around me, to shield me as we ran to get out of the cold and rain.

I rolled down the window and looked out at Finbar's premises. It was alive with lights and people. He'd created something from nothing. I had to admire him for that. The launch party had been a success, and when the photographs and story hit the papers, it would help establish his niche in the city.

Vaughn started up the car, and then something I'll never forget happened.

Finbar ran out of the bar into the street. 'Phred!' he shouted as we were about to drive off. 'I'd marry you tomorrow.'

For a second our eyes locked, acknowledging each other, then he turned and went back into the bar as we drove away.

Chapter Ten

One Year Later

I didn't see a lot of Finbar after that night. Not because he didn't like me, but because he did. Maybe that was Finbar's and my story. Meet briefly, then part for a year. Repeat every year. It had been a year since I'd seen him, at the launch party for his bar. He'd e–mailed once or twice, then that fizzled out.

So I was quite looking forward to seeing him again tonight at the premier of Bradley's new movie. Bradley had been nominated for a couple of awards for his performance in the film. This was a first. He'd never been nominated for any of his work before, but since he'd changed genres and gone for something different from his usual sci–fi, the nominations had been rolling in. And I'd been nominated for best screenplay. A lot had happened . . .

It was November. It hadn't snowed, but I

wished it would. I'd loved the icy landscape last year. But it was cold enough for snow. I could see my breath as I locked the house up for one of the last times. The lease was done. I'd tried to lease it, but the producer (snowman) said the property had been sold.

I was all dressed up for the premier — evening dress, sparkly shoes. I'd put a voluminous bag with some of my clothes into my car. Then I went in to have a last look around as it was, before I had to pack it all up and leave tomorrow. I'd wanted to say goodbye to the house myself. Vaughn had offered to come over, but sometimes in life the trip down memory lane is better walked on your own.

I'd wanted to remember all the times I'd had in this wonderful house. Vaughn said he'd help me pack it up in the morning.

Vaughn wanted me to move in with him. After the premier, I was going back to Vaughn's house. Maybe this was a sensible idea. If he could survive living with my writing, artwork, photography, martial arts, baking, dancing and dressmaking, maybe we had a long future together. Vaughn said he couldn't wait for me to move in. This was surely a great sign.

Vaughn and I had been dating for a year now. It didn't seem like that. Everything felt compressed into a shorter wavelength. I could still feel the snow from last November, the freezing air, skating in the park, working at the newspaper office. I felt as if suddenly, if it didn't work out with my scriptwriting, and I slid back down the slippery career slope, I could walk right back into the ringmaster's office and be the hoopla journalist I used to be.

There was something I still missed about working at the newspaper, despite having to economise with the heating on my old apartment, and Royce cracking the whip. I think I missed the sense of it. A newspaper office feels as if it will always be there. No matter what. There will always be journalists, subs and editors churning out the news as the world swirls around it. It smells of coffee and paper cups and ink that isn't really there. It feels like pressure and energy and a strange loyalty that binds it all together, and even people who don't get on join forces when the chips are down to churn out that paper no matter what. And I missed that.

Yes, they'd stolen my toffee, confiscated my hat, bet against me, ratted me out when the money was right, so . . . come to think of it . . .

As for the paparazzi, I'd hardly ever seen them in the newspaper office anyway. They were the phantoms who went out and found the gold dust shots, and e–mailed them in to the editors, negotiating prices depending on the quality of the carat. It was a whole different game getting out there and being part of them. An experience, I'll say that.

Scriptwriting is like the solitaire of the writing game. You're on your own. But I'm fine with that.

After Vaughn sold my script to a movie studio in Hollywood, there was increased interest in my work.

The producer (snowman) wanted to read

one of my scripts, so I gave him the one I'd written with Bradley in mind. Just as a spec script, a sample of what I could do. But he loved the script, and he bought it, and he pushed it through on a fast production schedule, filming for six months, post production two months, to have the premier one year from when he'd read it last November. They cast Bradley as the lead, and he was great. And that's why he was up for awards. Tonight was the New York premier.

After locking up my house, trying not to be sad about leaving it, I drove to Vaughn's house, and then he drove us in his car to the premier.

'It's snowing,' I said, peering out at the scene as he parked across the street from venue, the same one as last year.

I was excited about the premier.

Crowds of people were already there, along with press journalists and television news crews — and the paparazzi, cameras flashing, capturing the glitterati posing on the red carpet. The marquees dazzled with fairy lights, and I saw Bradley and his latest leading lady and 'friend' standing together in the spotlights. Bradley looked good. In the movie posters, the ripped leather gear and faux scar had been replaced by a gritty, cold–eyed spy, a classic figure set against a backdrop of a shadowy grey city. In real life, Bradley dressed to suit the mood of the movie in an immaculate black dinner suit, his blonde hair sleeked back emphasising his turquoise blue eyes. Go Bradley!

Vaughn and I stepped out of the car and headed across the street. Snow landed on my grey chiffon dress and grey velvet bolero, with the breeze blowing the long chiffon fabric like something out of a dream.

'You look wonderful,' Vaughn said.

I smiled at him. He looked great, with that handsome face, dark hair brushed back, grey eyes and a physique that made the most of his classic black dinner suit. Sometimes I wondered why Vaughn wasn't up there on the silver screen. He had the looks. Maybe the next script I wrote, I'd base the lead character on Vaughn.

Bradley was pleased to see us, and pulled me over to stand beside him for some of the photographs.

I blinked against the sea of flashing cameras, remembering how I'd flashed my pom poms last year. There were numerous paparazzi, and I wondered if any of them recognised me.

'Give us a flash of your tits, darlin',' one of them shouted. Well, that answered that question.

People were shouting to get Bradley's attention, but amid that I heard various male paparazzi voices commenting. I couldn't pick up every word, but I did hear sporadic words of encouragement . . .

'Boobs.'

'Knockers.'

'Flash your tits.'

'Pom poms.'

'Woolly hat.'

'Now she's rich.'

It had a certain ring to it. If it was set to music it could be quite a catchy little ditty.

Vaughn escorted me away, but not before the fracas erupted.

In the midst of the paparazzi melee, a scuffle seemed to have broken out. When I say seemed to, this was because with all the flashing cameras it was hard to tell exactly what was going on. I did hear the phrase . . .

'Soften your ribs for you.'

A couple of the media photographers were helped away, seemingly with softened ribs and sore faces. In the furore no one knew who'd punched them. It had all happened so fast.

From the back of the melee, a man emerged, wearing a black suit, black shirt and grey silk tie.

'Finbar!' I shouted.

He made his way through the paparazzi.

Vaughn gave me a look.

Now we knew the source of the scuffle. I hadn't wanted any trouble, but it was nice that he'd stuck up for me.

Finbar pushed his black hair back from his brow as he approached me. His quicksilver movements, a throwback to his boxing days, made him look sure footed and fit. He kissed my cheek and gave me a quick hug, his sparkling green eyes casting a glance at Vaughn to gauge his reaction.

Vaughn gave nothing away.

'You're looking well,' I said, thinking he appeared extra fit, well rested, and younger than he did a year ago. Any tiredness from the stress of setting up his pub had faded. I could sense Vaughn checking him out and coming to a similar conclusion.

'You too,' Finbar said. 'Beautiful dress. You look like a princess. And congratulations on all of this.' His eyes flicked around the premier setting, the fairy lights, crowds, glitz and celebrity.

'Thanks.'

'You deserve it all, Phred.'

He was moving, perpetual motion and energy sparking through him.

Vaughn put a possessive arm around my waist. 'People are going in now. We should go to our seats. You must be cold anyway.'

I wasn't cold at all, even in this floaty chiffon evening dress and snow sprinkled through the air.

Finbar took the hint. 'I'll see you inside,' he said to me, nodded curtly to Vaughn, and left us alone.

'I'll be back in a minute,' Vaughn said to me, and hurried after Finbar.

I heard part of their conversation.

'Keep your distance,' said Vaughn.

'I believe in fate,' Finbar said, 'and I just don't believe that you were put on this planet to be the man for Phred.'

'We're happy, so stay away from her,' said Vaughn. 'What we do is none of your business.'

'Phred loved me once. You can't change

that. She and I are connected from our pasts. Her happiness is my business.'

'You blew your chances with her,' said Vaughn.

'Indeed I did. Biggest mistake I ever made. Second biggest was not contacting her soon enough when I got to New York. What? You think I'm over here just because I want a pub in New York? I do want the pub, but I came here to win her back. But by that time, you'd already stepped in . . .'

I'd have heard more but I was distracted by the feeling of being watched. Someone in the crowd. I couldn't shake it off.

'. . . You're the same as me,' Finbar said to Vaughn. 'You're a salesman. I sell drink and a happy atmosphere. You sell people's talent to other people. That's all you do. You don't make anything. You don't contribute. Phred does. That makes you ordinary. She's anything but ordinary. Phred makes worlds. You're in Phred's world. Everything that's here tonight, is here because of her. I'll give Bradley his credit, he's turned into a fine actor. I've seen the trailers for this film. Bradley contributes. He brings the character to life, but it still comes from the world that Phred made.'

'I get what she does, and I care about her,' said Vaughn.

'I love Phred for herself. And so do you. But you also like her for how she makes you feel about yourself. I saw that in you last year. Working in pubs, you get to read people well. And she makes you feel better about yourself. But I want to make Phred feel better about *herself*.'

Vaughn repeated what he'd said, 'Keep your distance.'

Again, I felt I was being watched, scrutinised. I searched the faces in the crowd, trying to see past the flash of the cameras. And there he was. Standing back from everyone.

Royce.

I waved, and then walked away from the sparkle of the premier, across to where he stood in the street. He wore a traditional mackintosh, the raincoat making him look even more like an editor. He was still easy on the eye.

'Well done, Phred,' he said, giving me no time to respond. 'I wanted to give you this. I know you're about to go in and watch the movie. I hoped I'd see you in time.'

He handed me a small jewellery box. I opened it, and there was a diamond and silver brooch. A paparazzi camera brooch.

'It's beautiful,' I said, seeing it sparkle in the streetlight. A perfect little camera made from silver and diamonds, with one larger diamond set as the flash.

'I've never seen anything like this,' I said.

He held the box while I pinned it on my dress.

He smiled.

I cast a glance over at the premier. Vaughn was watching, an eager expression on his face.

'You'd better go,' Royce said.

I nodded and smiled, and then headed back across the street.

Royce called to me.

'Hey, Phred. It's not the same without you.'

'Is that offer of dinner still on?'

'I'll call you next week,' he said.

I nodded, and stepped back into the glare of the premier.

Vaughn didn't notice the brooch as we hurried to our seats in time for the movie starting. I'd asked that Finbar was invited to the premier, and so he was seated next to me on my left, with Vaughn on my right. The three of us were in the second row. Finbar and I were the only ones who'd bought sweets to eat during the movie. When Bradley realised we had sweets, he leaned back and helped himself to a few. He was in the first row in front of us. I even tempted Vaughn with a caramel.

'Where did the brooch come from?' Finbar whispered. 'You weren't wearing that earlier.'

'Royce gave it to me. He was waiting

outside.'

Finbar's eyes widened. 'Wonders will never cease.' Then he said, 'Though I'd still like to punch his lights out.'

'Ssh!' I said.

And then we all settled down to enjoy the movie.

The big premier party was at Bradley's house. We all headed there after watching the movie, which was a success with the audience if the cheers were anything to go by.

Hundreds of people were invited to the party, and Bradley had arranged for marquees to be set up in the garden. The snow was still falling, and everything was white and sparkling. There was catering, and bars with champagne cocktails, and dancing.

Finbar kept his distance, but occasionally he glanced over and gave me a reassuring wink that things were okay between us. I needed that. It could be another year before I met him again.

Vaughn was talking to a group of directors and producers, and I went to the buffet.

I was eating cake when Bradley called to me. 'Phred.' He came hurrying over. 'Let's go outside,' he said, talking hold of my hand and leading from the marquee to the front door entrance of his house. We sheltered from the snow, and both of us were lit up by the spotlights.

'I've wanted to talk to you in private all night,' he said.

'Is something wrong?'

'No, no, I just wanted you to know that I appreciate what you've done for me. Your script has given me the chance to show what I can do as an actor. From that very first night that I met you, in that freezing cold apartment of yours, you thought I could do better. And because of you, and your writing, I have.'

'I hope you win an award,' I said.

'I'll let you in on a secret. Because of how they have to film one of the awards events, I've been told that I have won.'

I cheered loudly.

'And I have a surprise for you.' He gave me an envelope from his jacket pocket.

I assumed it was money, a cheque.

'It's not money,' said Bradley.

I opened it, and there was a contract. I read it over. Bradley had bought the house that had been leased to me.

'It's yours now,' he said.

'The house?'

'I negotiated it as part of the deal with . . . the snowman . . . when I signed up to make the movie.'

'Oh Bradley, this is far too much. I can't take this —'

'Yes you can. No money actually exchanged hands. The producer was quite happy to include this in the deal. With all the property he has, he'll never miss one house.'

The realisation began to sink in. I had a house.

'Oh and, you didn't win the scriptwriting

award. You were second, Phred.'

'That's okay. Second's great. I have the house.' I couldn't stop smiling.

Bradley linked my arm through his, and we went back to the marquee.

'Remember, don't tell anyone about the award's outcome yet.'

I nodded. 'Can I tell them about the house?'

He smiled. 'Hell, yes.'

Vaughn was the first one I told.

'Bradley sort of bought my house. It was part of the movie deal with the snowman producer. Bradley's giving the house to me for making him into an award nominated actor.' I was careful not to say award winner, but I think Vaughn knew.

He was delighted for me. I think.

'You'll still come and live with me though,' he said.

'Yes, but I won't have to pack everything up from my house. I'll live between the two houses. I have plans.'

Vaughn smiled, cupped my face in his hands and kissed me. 'I don't doubt it.' Then he became serious. 'I know how Finbar feels about you, and that he'll always be waiting for you, but that doesn't mean I feel any less. We're just different men. I think I can make you happy if you'll give me a chance.'

I kissed him. 'I am happy with you.' I was. I had loved Finbar, and I still had strong feelings for him, but the scars of the past still cut deep. He'd dumped me in Dublin, and I hadn't quite gotten over that. I knew I would, but just not yet.

Vaughn wrapped me in his strong embrace. 'I have to go to Hollywood tomorrow night. I thought perhaps you'd like to come with me this time.'

'To Hollywood?'

'Yes, you can catch some sun, relax by the pool and eat cake.'

'I haven't dived in two or three years,' I said.

'Dived?'

'High dived off the board into a swimming pool,' I explained. 'I used to love diving into the Irish Sea.'

'Well, I hope Hollywood is ready for you.'

I looked out at the snow, and I guess he read my thoughts.

'We'll be gone for a few days,' he said. 'The snow will still be here when you get back.'

And it was.

Hollywood was an experience. Fascinating how all the networking goes on. Vaughn secured deals for his clients while we were there.

I got some writing done. I was working on two new scripts. One was the sequel to Bradley's movie. They wanted another adventure for his spy character, so I was working on that. And a romantic comedy. I was giving that a go.

However, a lot of the time I was in the

swimming pool. I often had it all to myself. Not that it was quiet. People sat around the edges on loungers. The women had their hairs done and make up on, very glam. I could see why they wouldn't be interested in doing back flips off the high board. I tried not to splash.

After a few days of diving, I felt better than ever, and fit as a butcher's dog.

Vaughn liked me in my little silver and gold bikinis, and seemed happy to ogle me rather than the other gorgeous women.

So now we were back in New York.

I'd headed into Manhattan which was a dazzling winter landscape again. I was having lunch with Royce, and I'd worn the paparazzi camera brooch.

As I was early, I decided to go skating on one of the outdoor rinks.

I was warmly dressed, with a woolly hat, and a scarf that I'd pinned with the brooch Royce gave me. It sparkled in the light.

I put my skates on, and skated on to the ice. The snow felt wonderful, the air cold and fresh. I loved the sound of the blades on the ice.

Attempting too many spins, my lace came loose, and I went to the edge of the rink to tie it.

The skate hire lady smiled. ‘Ooh, cute brooch. Does it represent something?’

‘Yes,’ I said. ‘I used to be one of the paparazzi.’

www.ingramcontent.com/pod-product-compliance
Ingram Content Group UK Ltd.
Pitfield, Milton Keynes, MK11 3LW, UK
UKHW020133250726
13967UKWH00002B/619